COLLECTING

Small Silverware

Two late Victorian circular scent bottles and a selection of earlier pieces including an
unmarked articulated fish scent flask c. 1780 and a selection of four snuff boxes.

COLLECTING

Small Silverware

Stephen Helliwell

PHAIDON · CHRISTIE'S
OXFORD

Phaidon·Christie's Limited
Littlegate House
St Ebbe's Street
Oxford
OX1 1SQ

First published 1988

British Library Cataloguing in Publication Data:

Helliwell, Stephen
    Collecting Small Silverware
    1. Silverware———England———Collectors
    and collecting
    I. Title
    739.2'37'42   NK7143

ISBN 0-7148-8047-7

Printed in Spain by Heraclio Fournier SA, Vitoria

Contents

Preface 7

1 Collecting and Caring for Silver 9

2 Cutlery 31

3 Further Dining-Room Silver 61

4 Alcoholic Antiques 76

5 Bedroom and Bathroom Silver 93

6 Desk Equipment and Accessories 107

7 The Tobacco Trade 128

8 Personal Possessions 147

9 Silver for Children 169

Bibliography 185

Glossary 187

Index 189

For my parents, with gratitude for
their support in the early days

Preface

In the past silver was prized primarily as a material for the manufacture of coinage or household objects. Once credited with almost mystical qualities, although silver has been valued for thousands of years collecting it is a comparatively new phenomenon. The relative rarity of the precious ore, the dangers involved in mining, and the skill required for working the metal, have combined to ensure that it is still highly sought after. Moreover, the malleability of the metal has enabled silversmiths to create an enormous array of objects, from the functional to the magnificent, using many different techniques. Silver can be cast, rolled, hammered, and even drawn out into wire, articles can then be engraved, chased, embossed, etched, and enamelled.

Many of these items are of great beauty, and one can find a host of references to silver in old diaries and letters, recording the delight with which our ancestors greeted new designs or particularly fine workmanship. Nevertheless, objects fashioned in silver were valued primarily for their bullion value. Compact, if somewhat heavy, they were easily portable in times of trouble. Alternatively, they could be hidden away. Pepys's diaries record that he buried his silver in the garden, as the Great Fire of London swept ever nearer to his house in 1666. Silver was seen as a good investment, as it could be melted down into coins or pawned quite easily, should the owner fall on hard times. Another advantage was that old pieces could be adapted to 'modern' styles, and many wealthy people sent their family plate to be scrapped, the silversmiths reworking the metal and charging only for their labour and the cost of smelting. Such was the fate of many large articles, but fortunately countless smaller pieces have survived. These were not worth melting down because of their lack of weight.

The Victorians too adapted antique silver to their own tastes. The vandalism of later-chasing was widespread throughout the last century (see page 24). At the turn of the century however, people increasingly began to recognize the beauty of old silver. Simple and humble pieces, once despised, began to find favour again, and silversmiths started to reproduce the designs of the past, making many fine copies of eighteenth century and earlier pieces.

Today, of course, there is much to stimulate the passionate collector. The media delight in reporting ever-spiralling prices, and there are a number of excellent reference books and magazines, as well as specialist clubs covering diverse subjects such as wine labels and even button hooks. Our appetites are whetted further by programmes such as 'The Antiques Roadshow', one of the most popular and entertaining programmes on British television.

People begin to collect silver for many reasons. Some may be started off by a gift or an inheritance, while others simply become interested in the hallmarks on family pieces, exploring the intricacies of the tiny punches with an old magnifying glass. Many buy purely for investment, although few can resist the charm of antique silver for long, personal taste gradually outweighing financial consideration to some extent. Obviously, while every buyer hopes that he has made a wise choice, mistakes are inevitable. Nevertheless, I hope that this book will help keep them to a minimum, providing a useful guide aimed both at those who are just starting out on an absorbing and fascinating hobby, and at more experienced collectors who perhaps feel the need to branch out into new fields of exploration.

The prices given in this book are simply guides of retail costs. I have suggested wide ranges to allow for the differences between good and bad objects, and between the various sources of antique silver (see page 14) available to the collector. Throughout the years that I have been studying and collecting silver, there have been few great leaps or slumps in value. On the whole, prices have remained very stable, so I hope that those quoted here will be of use for several years to come.

1 Collecting and Caring for Silver

Styles and Marks of Old Silver

Over the many years of silver manufacture, styles have changed enormously, following the influences of varying cultures and numerous shifts in power. British silver design was swayed by fashions on the continent, the well-travelled rich introducing new shapes and styles of decoration which were gradually assimilated into the rest of society. The late seventeenth and early eighteenth centuries were marked by the influence of Huguenot craftsmen fleeing persecution in their native France. Many arrived in Britain, challenging the established silversmiths who were eventually forced to adapt to new designs.

Changes in style seem to have occured every thirty years or so, fashions going from one extreme to the other, as if the buyer has become bored with one style, rejecting it completely in favour of a total contrast in shape and decoration. Fortunately, even the most humble silver objects were influenced by new fashions, although, in many cases, they were toned down to satisfy the more conservative clients. As a result the collector can build up a comprehensive picture of the evolution of styles, with the aid of small and often inexpensive objects.

Silver objects made before 1700 are, on the whole, very scarce, as so many have been melted down for currency or for the creation of new pieces. Examples can be seen in museums, but the modern collector is unlikely to be able to buy such early pieces, unless he has almost unlimited funds. As this book is designed to cover affordable silver objects, these costly pieces have been omitted so that the reader can concentrate on those which are still readily available. These date from the beginning of the eighteenth century, when most silver was heavy in decoration, with cut-card work, fluting, and gadrooning applied to basically simple shapes. The result was very pleasing, and, moreover, the craftsmanship of this period excellent.

In the 1730s a new fashion was introduced from France. Characterized by an overwhelming mass of disorganized and unbalanced decoration, often incorporating shells and scrolls, this contrasting style, the rococo, swept through the country, replacing the splendid simplicity which had gone before. The basic shapes of objects changed and curved

1 William and Mary dressing table set with simple, elegant lines and fine engraving, by Anthony Nelme, London 1691. Typical of the sturdy silver made in the early eighteenth century, it would now be very costly. £30,000-£50,000.

2 Selection of Georgian bonbon dishes, the smallest example made in London 1756, with hand-sawn rococo scrolls and flowers and a chased rococo cartouche. The slightly later basket on the extreme left was also hand-pierced, although its decoration is more regular. Nevertheless, the cartouche is still rococo in style. The other baskets display typical neo-classical decoration, with beading, swags, and paterae, and bright-cut engraving. All three were made in the 1780s, using the cheaper technique of machine piercing. £500–£600 each.

lines were introduced wherever possible, creating a new fluidity of design.

Fashions changed again with the introduction of the neo-classical in the 1760s. Inspired by visits to Italy, influential designers such as Robert Adam based the new style firmly on the architecture of the Greeks and Romans. Symmetrical and balanced, light and delicate, it can be seen as a complete contrast with the rococo of the previous generation.

At the end of the eighteenth century the neo-classical began to lose favour, particularly as workmanship had begun to deteriorate, with the introduction of cheaper mass-production methods. It was now considered cold and insipid, and more flamboyance was demanded by the rich. Thus, the regency style was introduced, with its opulence, heaviness, and fine workmanship. Gilding became popular at this time, and 'historicism' spread rapidly, resulting in the manufacture of silver in a curious combination of styles inspired by ancient Greece, Rome and Egypt, and the Orient.

It is difficult to identify one style as being more popular than any other during the reign of Queen Victoria. Many silversmiths made reproductions or adaptations of earlier designs, generally creating pieces which were far more ostentatious than the originals they copied. Simplicity was shunned as silver had become a status symbol, rather than a medium for the manufacture of everyday objects. Every surface was now smothered with chased decoration, usually incorporating scrolling plants. Thus, the style of naturalism was born in the 1840s. The Victorians also loved novelty, and their silversmiths were kept busy supplying condiments in the form of animals, cabbage leaf plates, and other nonsensical pieces.

3 Two early nineteenth-century salts formed from thick sheet metal. Heavy in design, but of fine quality. They are illustrated with a George III rococo salt, with hand-pierced sides. *Left* to *Right:* Paul Storr, London, 1817, £300-£400; Daniel Pontifex, London, 1806, £200-£250; Robert and David Hennell, London, 1765, £120-£160. Pairs of salt cellers are much more expensive than single examples.

By the 1870s many people were tired of this relentlessly elaborate style, and looked elsewhere for inspiration. They found it in Japan, and a new, 'aesthetic' type of decoration based loosely on Japanese art was introduced. Light and airy, this soon evolved into the Art Nouveau movement, characterized by gentle, sinuous, elongated lines suggesting stylized plant forms, a 'hand-made' quality (often completely spurious), and the reintroduction of enamels.

During the early twentieth century the Art Nouveau style began to deteriorate. Designs became increasingly insipid, and new and exciting styles were sought. This demand accelerated after the First World War, the disillusioned seeking a completely contrasting, more positive life-style, with artifacts to match. They found it in Art Deco, a style named after the 1925 Paris exhibition. Powerful, angular shapes and strong

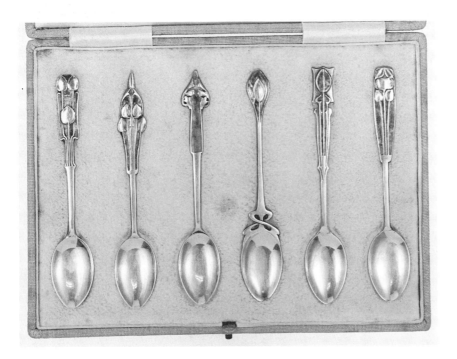

4 Liberty and Co. teaspoons, made in Birmingham 1900. Enhanced by blue and green enamelling and with decoration inspired by plant forms, each member of the set is different. £600-£800.

enamel or celluloid colours were combined effectively, creating a strong, functional quality. Much collected today, Art Deco silver can be more expensive than early eighteenth-century silver, despite its comparatively recent manufacture.

Changes of style in silver can be a useful guide to dating and identification. One must, however, remember that some designs became fashionable again many years after their first appearance. The Victorians and Edwardians were particularly fond of reproduction silver, often of the finest quality. One must also bear in mind that new styles might not reach provincial or colonial silversmiths for several years. The Victorians were influenced by trade exhibitions like the Great Exhibition of 1851, and by popular 'art journals' which laid down rules for home interiors and artifacts, but our earlier ancestors had far fewer guide lines. The majority travelled rarely in their own countries, let alone abroad, and consequently were much less influenced by new fashions in decoration.

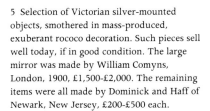

5 Selection of Victorian silver-mounted objects, smothered in mass-produced, exuberant rococo decoration. Such pieces sell well today, if in good condition. The large mirror was made by William Comyns, London, 1900, £1,500-£2,000. The remaining items were all made by Dominick and Haff of Newark, New Jersey, £200-£500 each.

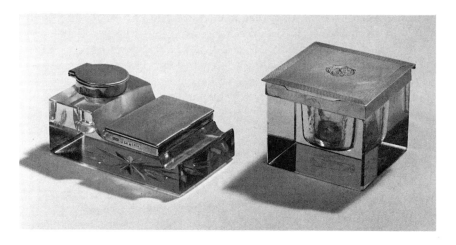

6 The 1920s saw the introduction of Art Deco designs, with straight lines and geometric, engine-turned decoration. *Left:* J.G. and S., Birmingham, 1922, £150-£200; *Right:* Walker and Hall, Sheffield, 1930, £80-£120.

As a result silver manufactured in small, isolated towns may well be more than twenty years behind that made in sophisticated London, New York, or Boston.

While one can soon learn to recognize typical styles and shapes, linking them to certain periods of manufacture, it is unlikely that anyone will be able to learn all of the various marks employed by British and American silversmiths. There are simply too many to memorize, and both dealers and collectors with many years of experience will need to resort to reference books. You will find a list of these in the bibliography. Eventually one will start to recognize date letters and town marks, and the marks of certain makers. One should always check back to the hallmarks for accurate dating, although these can be misleading, as explained on page 21.

Buying and Selling

There are many sources of old silver which the collector can explore, ranging from the top auction houses and dealers, some of which are now household names, to locally advertised flea markets held in town halls and scout huts. This section will contain both general advice, and an examination of the pros and cons of the various outlets.

The most important thing to remember is that one should never be afraid to ask advice. One can usually make a personal contact, even in the most inhibiting premises, and a friend on the other side of the counter is often very useful, pointing out repairs for example or recommending reliable restorers. Auction house porters are often very knowledgeable, steering the beginner away from poor specimens and advising on realistic bids where no estimates are given.

Many dealers are delighted to contact clients who are looking for specific objects, sometimes even taking a smaller profit in the knowledge that a rapid sale will almost certainly take place. Auctioneers offer the same service, but remember that it is worth the cost of having cards printed. A telephone call from the trade can save you a lot of time and effort, and addresses written on scruffy scraps of paper usually get lost or forgotten. One should also build up a collection of dealers' business cards, keeping a record of those who have been useful in the past.

Remember too the basic equipment: a pocket guide to hallmarks and a good magnifying glass. The latter are quite expensive and most people are loath to lend them to strangers, as they seem to have a habit of disappearing! If you are trying to build up a set of cutlery, then you should also carry a tape measure and a picture of the pattern you are collecting, along with the measurements of the various pieces you need. Even standard designs of flatware can vary, and it is annoying to find that a new addition to one's set does not quite match in size or shape.

Always be prepared to bargain. Although there is nothing more annoying than customers who ask for 'trade terms', when it is quite obvious that they are buying in a private capacity, haggling is now accepted in most retail establishments, and many dealers will automatically offer a small discount if they feel that you are on the brink of purchase. However, if the dealer says that he is offering his lowest possible price, then it is polite to believe him. Few dealers make vast profits, and premises and other overheads can eat into them, particularly if a certain item fails to sell for a while, thus tying up capital. If a piece seems too expensive, then leave it for someone else. After all, it may still be there on a subsequent visit, with a lower price tag.

Specialist collectors should investigate whether there is a club which covers their particular interest. Much knowledge can be gleaned from other members or from the news-sheets, and there is also the possibility that swaps or sales of duplicates can be arranged. Some clubs even organize trips abroad to see private collections, while others hold auctions or publish advertisements, neither of which are available to non-members.

7 A hectic morning view at Christie's of South Kensington, London, as potential buyers examine both silver and plate before calculating their bids. Approximately three hundred lots are sold each week by this saleroom alone. Many of them cost less than £200 each, making them ideal for the new collector.

8 Mary Cooke Antiques of King Street, London, a shop specializing in silver collectables, with an ever-changing stock of small pieces such as snuff boxes and wine labels on display.

When buying, most collectors start at the lower end of the market, visiting small antique fairs and even car-boot sales. These can be great fun, and may also reveal the occasional rarity, but require plenty of time and energy. All too often there will be nothing of interest, although you can find them ideal for small and inexpensive pieces which smarter establishments may scorn. Street markets are also lively places, some catering for serious collectors while others are geared primarily to the tourist. The main disadvantage of both types of venue is their erratic nature. One may find that dealers simply disappear after a few weeks, many going away to stock up on goods. Others may leave for more sinister reasons, as street markets are sometimes used for the disposal of stolen goods. While most stall-holders are perfectly respectable, the odd rogue may be on the look out for unsuspecting buyers to sell them fakes or damaged pieces.

Permanent markets are more reliable, and there are several which specialize in silver. The London Silver Vaults in Chancery Lane and The Bond Street Silver Galleries in New Bond Street are two such markets, each containing many different units with a wide variety of stock. Although the beginner may find the amount of silver on display some-what intimidating, prices in these specialist markets are generally very competitive.

There are many shops which deal solely in antique silver. These vary enormously, some offering fine pieces of museum quality and rarity, while others handle more ordinary and affordable specimens. The most 'exclusive' are often disheartening places at first but once one is known, then barriers start to fall. Good customers can be offered excellent discounts, and there may also be an understanding that purchases can be returned at a later date, the shop refunding the price and even giving a profit on some occasions. Some shops will even hold goods on approval, offering credit terms to well-known customers. Restoration will be clearly marked on the price ticket and is usually of the finest quality, many shops jealously guarding the skilful silversmiths they have managed to find. Sadly the price itself is often written in a code, a practice which ensures that browsers are not really made to feel welcome. Obviously shops want their wares to attract customers, and as a result one may find that pieces have been over-cleaned and restored. Old silver should look old, and there is little point in giving it a machine-buffed, brand-new finish. Fortunately, today most dealers recognize the value of patina, and the days of the over-bright and sparkling antique seem to be numbered.

Lastly, the collector may decide to tackle the auction rooms, cutting out the middle man and his profits. Once again, these can seem rather daunting, although no-one need fear that a sneeze or a scratch of the nose will buy an expensive lot! There is usually plenty of time to view the goods, and one should always invest in a catalogue, marking it clearly with distinct upper limits. Codes look very impressive, but many auctioneers sell quickly, leaving no time to decide whether XYZ means £100 or £150. Never buy on impulse, but always view thoroughly. 'Auction fever' can affect the most level-headed person. A lot which appears to be selling very cheaply may look fine from a distance but closer examination can reveal a multitude of faults. Few auction catalogues mention damage or restoration, and the collector must ascertain for himself the true value of the pieces in which he is interested. Many auctioneers publish estimates in their catalogues, but these should be treated as a rough guide rather than taken as an accurate picture of the eventual hammer price. Getting to know the saleroom porter can help enormously. After all, he sees similar lots sold every week, and will know what is to come up for sale in the near future. He may steer you clear of second-rate pieces in the knowledge that better examples will appear in subsequent sales.

Bidding is great fun, although the beginner may be somewhat puzzled by the leaps in price which the auctioneer calls out. The majority of salerooms increase their bids by roughly ten per cent, starting off an item worth £100 at about £50. After a certain level has been reached, then bidding will usually rise in the ratio of 2, 5, 8 and 10. Thus, a piece may start at £200, with subsequent bids of £220, £250, £280, £300 and so on. It is a good idea to attend several sales before attempting to bid, thus gaining total familiarity with this system. If you are unable to attend a particular sale, then the auction house will execute bids on your behalf, buying as cheaply as possible against the bidders present in the room. One can also leave bids with saleroom porters. If, at the last minute, you decide to go to the sale in person then you must cancel any bids left with the saleroom or porter. Failure to do this can result in bidding against yourself; a sure way of paying too much.

Do bear in mind that you may have to pay more than the hammer price. Most salerooms now have a buyers' premium, this worked out as a percentage of the price bid for each lot. VAT is then added onto the premium, so a £100 lot may eventually cost you £111.50 (£100 hammer price plus ten per cent buyers' premium plus fifteen per cent VAT). There may be other charges, and the prospective buyer should read the catalogue carefully. For example, if the lots are being sold on behalf of a dealer, then the saleroom may collect VAT for him. Each lot affected in this way will be clearly marked.

Perhaps the main advantage of the auction houses is that they normally sell pieces exactly as they come in, with no over-zealous cleaning. One soon learns to see the beauty which may lie behind many years of tarnish and neglect. There is, however, a serious drawback, particularly relevant to the collector of small, inexpensive items. Many salerooms have large overheads, and as a result are forced to lot pieces together, usually aiming at a minimum lot value of at least £100. Thus, the buyer who wishes to purchase a single pair of sugar tongs may also end up with a miscellaneous collection of less interesting pieces. These can often be re-entered for sale, although there is always the risk that prices may become less buoyant. Moreover, one must then pay the sellers' commission.

There may well come a time when the collector wishes to sell some pieces. With luck these will be sold at a profit, so keeping up with inflation at least. In all probability, however, some items will be sold at a small loss, creating a 'swings and roundabouts' situation.

The best prices for unwanted pieces are probably to be achieved by selling directly to other collectors, either by advertising or by building up a circle of acquaintances interested in the same areas. Alternatively, one may decide to rent a stall at an antiques fair or a 'pitch' at a car-boot sale. The latter is particularly useful for the disposal of the lower-priced items which inevitably seem to build up over a long period of collecting. If you hire a stall at a fair, then always check whether tables and lighting are provided. Be prepared for the possibility that a certain amount of pilfering may take place. It is difficult to keep an eye on small pieces, so glass-topped cabinets are a good idea.

Some people cannot cope with selling, as it requires a certain amount of nerve combined with an extrovert nature! As a result, they opt to sell to the trade. Generally one will obtain a lower price this way, as the dealer has to make a profit to live. Another option is to sell at auction, although the results may be somewhat disappointing. Most buyers at auction are, once again, dealers who will bid with their eventual profit in mind. Private buyers are now visiting the salerooms in larger numbers, however, and as a result prices can soar way above the estimates fixed by their staff. While you can always place a reserve on your property, some salerooms charge a commission if the piece fails to sell. This is normally calculated at five per cent of the price, and covers the cost of printing, staffing and storage. Obviously this charge must be remembered by the seller who hopes to achieve a profit.

This short guide to buying and selling will be particularly useful to those just beginning to collect antique silver. The most important piece of advice which must be remembered at all times is never be too afraid or embarrassed to ask a question, whether in a shop or in an auction gallery. This may avoid expensive and frustrating mistakes, and should lead to the creation of a worthwhile collection which will give much pleasure over the years.

Potential Problems . . . Repairs and Fakes

All collectors of antique and second-hand silver will come across problematical pieces in their search for attractive specimens at affordable prices. One must bear in mind that the majority of items described in this book are not rare. As a result the buyer can afford to be patient, rejecting damaged or repaired pieces in the knowledge that better specimens will eventually appear on the market.

One type of damage common to all objects of old silver is the removal of unwanted inscriptions. These may well have been obliterated when the object was sold, few buyers wanting someone else's initials as a constant reminder that they have bought second-hand silver. Inscriptions can be removed in three ways. Firstly, one might ask a silversmith to erase them using a polishing machine. This results in the creation of a weak and thin patch of silver which can be felt by pressing the metal gently with one's thumbs. Any sponginess should warn the prospective buyer against purchase. Inscriptions might also be filled with a flood of solder, the surface smoothed down afterwards. This method is more difficult to detect, although differences in colour or patina might lead to suspicion. The most obvious way of concealing an unwanted inscription is to solder a thin silver plate or cartouche over the offending patch. Although the silversmiths went to much trouble, attempting to hide the edges by buffing them down against the original surface, one can normally detect a slight ridge with one's finger nails. This technique seems to have been practised primarily on snuff boxes and other small pieces, their thin gauge of silver making erasure an impractical solution.

One may also come across the phenomenon of later engraving, used to enhance the value of perfectly ordinary objects. The names and crests of famous people are added, the clumsy forger paying little attention to accuracy. For example, I have seen two salvers engraved: 'From Lord Nelson to Lady Hamilton', each one made over twenty years after the death of the supposed donor! Such forgeries are easy to spot of course, but others are more difficult to recognize, so be cautious of all engraving, particularly if a celebrity is mentioned. Over-sharp engraving should also be treated with scepticism, especially if it is found on a piece which otherwise shows all the expected signs of wear.

If a rare but damaged piece is essential to a collection, filling a gap in terms of style or date, the buyer should be aware of the problems and costs involved to have it repaired. Skilful silversmiths are difficult to find, as most work primarily for the trade. Many are simply not interested in small, private jobs, and those who are may have a long waiting list. Moreover, an apparently simple job can often involve several hours of work on the part of the silversmith, and may subsequently cost considerably more than anticipated. It is always better if you can contact a silversmith directly to discuss the work. While many jewellers and antique dealers are quite happy to organize repairs on your behalf, they will normally charge a commission to cover their time and trouble. A direct approach should save a few pounds, and will also give you the opportunity to examine the quality of work. A committed craftsman will be delighted to show off his talents and may well explain how he proposes to tackle the problem.

Fakes made from silver have been in circulation almost as long as silversmiths have been producing genuine articles. Sub-standard pieces have long been a problem in Britain, and the use of 'drossie rubbage and refuse metall' ('Anatomy of Abuses in England' by Philip Stubbes, 1408) by unscrupulous manufacturers to adulterate silver was widespread, leading to the introduction of hallmarking laws to protect the buyer. Despite these regulations, many dubious pieces were still produced, particularly after the reintroduction of a duty on silver submitted for assay, in 1784. This was calculated at sixpence per ounce, increasing the price of larger items quite considerably. Many manufacturers submitted small items to the hall, paying only a negligible amount of duty. These pieces would then be destroyed, their marks cut out and then soldered into much bigger items.

Today such 'duty dodgers' can often be recognized by the arrangement of their hallmarks. Most are grouped in a circle, this revealing that they were removed from a watch case, although in some cases pieces of flatware were submitted for assay, their punches arranged in a straight line. Careful examination may reveal lines of solder surrounding the 'sweated in' marks, these usually quite obvious if one breathes out onto the suspect item, particularly if it is tarnished.

'Duty dodgers' are quite genuine pieces, in that they were made during the correct period, often by skilful silversmiths who simply tried to avoid the duty payable on silver. In most cases the metal they used

9 Sturdy eighteenth-century mug, with a totally plain body, and a similarly shaped mug made in the same year, 1772. While the former is in original condition, the latter has been decorated by a nineteenth-century silversmith, with hand-chased arabesques and a vignette of a fisherman. Both examples are four and a half inches high. The plain mug would now sell for £600-£800, while the later-decorated specimen would retail for £300-£400.

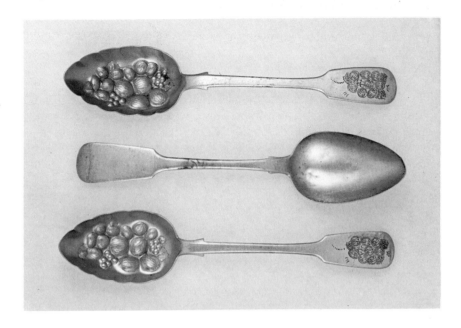

10 'Berry' or fruit spoons cost twice as much as plain tablespoons. Many were decorated by hand with flowers and fruit in the nineteenth century. This work is still done today, usually with a stamping machine. Fortunately, plain flatware is still commonly available, so little harm comes of this practice. The above spoons were all made by William Eley and William Fearn, London, 1825.

11 Perhaps the commonest alteration of all: a cream jug made from a christening mug, the added spout cutting right through the reeded decoration. Such pieces cannot be sold legally in Britain, unless the spout is tested and then hallmarked if 'up to scratch'. Large numbers of mugs were ruined in this way during the last century.

was up to standard. Regrettably, once antique silver became collected, there were, and indeed still are, many fakes made deliberately to deceive.

One method of copying old silver is to take castings from genuine pieces. This in itself is not illegal, but if the silversmith also casts the antique hallmarks, then he is breaking the law. Cast marks can often be detected by close examination with a jeweller's glass, the high magnification revealing granulations or marks left by the sand commonly used in the casting process. Pieces reproduced using the lost wax method of casting are more difficult to recognize. There will be no tell-tale granulations, although one may sometimes see tiny air bubbles. Sets of items cast from the same original can be spotted quite easily however. Each piece is identical, the spurious hallmarks all in the same place, along with any areas of wear or damage.

Another method of deceiving was by stamping the piece with home-made punches, these producing 'antique' marks with varying degrees of accuracy. Many were quite crude but some were amazingly realistic, and the collector has to use experience to assess whether the date indicated by the hallmark is confirmed by the style of the article in question.

New pieces of silver may be inset with marks taken from genuine antique pieces, these either of small value or too badly damaged to be repaired and sold. As mentioned earlier, these marks may well be arranged in a different pattern from that which one would normally expect. Often the marks are out of proportion to the piece in which they have been set, the assay offices usually using larger punches for bigger items.

Hallmarks were often stamped very heavily and examination of the interior of a genuine piece should reveal small dents where the punches

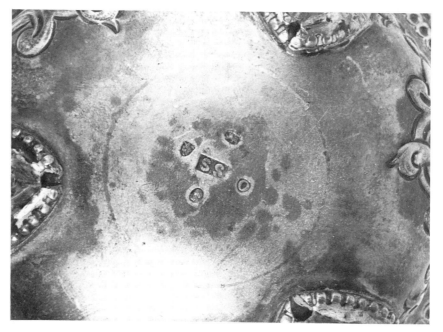

12 Curious bonbon dish with George III marks. The piece is ugly and unbalanced both in shape and decoration. A quick look at the bottom of the bowl reveals that it is a fake, with inset marks probably taken from a watch case. One can see the line of solder surrounding the patch quite easily. While this could be disguised with one of the new plating liquids, the swing handle is not marked at all. This alone should be enough to deter the prospective buyer.

have distorted the soft metal. If a piece bears no dents, then it is possible that a whole false bottom or plate has been soldered in. Solder marks will not show, as they are sandwiched between the genuine and the false bottom, the outside join usually concealed by the addition of a pedestal foot or a frieze of cast decoration. Pieces with added bottoms often sound rather 'tinny' when tapped, and may feel surprisingly light, their apparently solid and thick bottoms actually made from two much thinner plates with a space in between.

Applied hallmarks may also show signs of wear incompatible with their position. Punches hidden away beneath the foot of an article would normally be quite crisp, as most people cleaning silver tend to forget those areas which are not on view. Worn marks in such a position should arouse suspicion, as indeed should perfect marks on an otherwise worn object. The modern collector takes great care to avoid damaging the marks on old silver (see page 25), but in the past pieces were made to be used, and few, if any, butlers would have thought to protect the punches in their efforts to clean silver quickly and efficiently.

One must always remember that each detachable piece of silver should have a mark matching those on the main body of the piece. Thus, the lid of a teapot or a coffee-pot should be stamped at least with a lion passant mark, most examples also bearing the maker's mark. The same would also apply to candlestick nozzles and snuffers, vesta case lids, snuff box lids, and to every other piece of silver. Articles may also have been created from an entirely different object. Mugs were often stretched to form coffee pots, while tapersticks might be created from wine funnel stands. In both cases only the main body of the piece will be marked, thus warning the collector against purchase, even if the price seems very reasonable.

Early spoons are prime targets for the faker. Some are simply cast from originals, but in most cases genuine pieces of old silver are converted by the addition of cast apostle terminals. I have seen many examples of mid to late eighteenth-century cutlery with these spurious additions. Such fakes are easy to recognize, their hallmarks giving the game away. These indicate manufacture many years after apostle spoons went out of fashion. The rarity of early eighteenth-century forks has also led to many fakes. The bowls of genuine trefid-end or dognose pattern spoons are hammered flat and then reshaped, each being cut into the requisite three prongs. Vast numbers of spoons were ruined in this way, as collectors sought to assemble complete canteens of cutlery. Fortunately, detection is again quite easy, as the prongs of converted forks feel too sharp, and lack the spring of their genuine counterparts.

Finally, many reproductions in the Queen Anne style were made in Britannia Standard silver, particularly in the late nineteenth and early

13 These four apostle spoons were manufactured from George III tablespoons made in London, 1792. By this time, spoons with cast terminals had become old-fashioned, and flatware makers were concentrating on new styles with broad, flat handles. Close examination reveals that all four terminals are identical, as each one was cast from the same mould. They were then soldered onto the ends of late eighteenth-century spoons, creating forgeries designed to attract the unwary collector.

twentieth centuries when such copies were very fashionable. Many of the later copies are of impressive quality and weight, factors which are reflected in high prices today. It is easy to render such items even more valuable, by removing their modern date letters and makers' marks with the aid of a polishing machine. The Britannia Standard marks will be left untouched, thus implying an extra couple of centuries of antiquity. These fakes can be difficult to spot, and the optimistic collector may well be fooled by the excellent workmanship of some turn-of-the-century silversmiths.

Apart from deliberate fakes, many items of antique silver have been altered in the past, our ancestors commissioning the conversion of old fashioned pieces into more useful objects. Thus, mugs were given spouts to form milk jugs and pap boats were given legs to create sauce boats. Many wealthy households owned large stocks of massive plates and platters and when porcelain superceded silver for table services much of this silver was simply melted down or adapted into other objects. Plates were converted into salvers and bowls, their reshaping usually distorting the hallmarks which today act as a warning to the careful buyer. Silver with later additions cannot be sold legally in Britain, unless the additions are tested by an assay office. If they are 'up to scratch' they can be marked, but if the added metal is of insufficient quality, then the antique marks on the original item must be obliterated.

Ideas of what is pleasing to the eye change from generation to generation, and much early silver was vandalized beyond recognition by collectors who scorned the plain and simple. In particular, the majority of Victorian collectors combined their taste for 'the antique' with the craze for decoration, and many pieces of plain silver were ruined by the addition of chasing, embossing, and engraving. Mugs particularly were victims of this, and one can still find many examples highly decorated with farmyard and pastoral scenes, or with vigourous and detailed battles, their original lovely simple lines now lost for ever.

The workmanship of the Victorian silversmiths can usually not be faulted, and one can only regret that their clients chose to combine antique hallmarks with typically nineteenth-century exuberance, instead of ordering the manufacture of entirely new articles. Although later-decorated pieces can be sold legally, as no new metal was used in their creation, they are, understandably, far less popular with the majority of modern collectors. Generally they will sell for about half the price of a plain original. Occasionally a piece of silver is 'de-chased', its later decoration removed by skilful hammering in an attempt to recreate the original plain and more valuable object. Such pieces are usually somewhat distorted in appearance, as the silver in their bodies has been stretched twice. Close examination will reveal traces of the decoration which has been removed, and the metal itself will feel spongy and soft when slight pressure is applied.

I hope that this brief outline of the potential pitfalls will not deter the budding collector. One may wonder whether it is still possible to find any decent, original pieces, but they are certainly still around in large numbers. Experience is essential, and one should try to see and handle as much antique silver as possible, either in museums or in shops and auction rooms. Eventually anyone with a notion of beauty and symmetry will begin to 'feel' that a piece is wrong, even if he cannot say exactly what has happened to it at some stage of its life. This 'sixth sense' should never be ignored, as mistakes may prove to be expensive, leaving the collector with an unattractive piece which will be a constant source of dissatisfaction.

Caring for and Displaying Small Silver

Today clear marks are of paramount importance to the modern collector. Despite the modern obsession with preserving antique hallmarks however, it is important to clean silver. Tarnished, it has a dead and sad appearance, but once cleaned it comes to life, sparkling in the light in a most attractive way. This chapter will explain the best methods of cleaning silver without harming the material itself, as well as discussing methods of maintaining the brilliance for a certain period of time.

Silver is a comparatively soft metal, and constant and over-enthusiastic cleaning will eventually wear away the all-important marks, as well as any engraved or chased decoration. Over the years many pieces have been ruined, their silver worn away, particularly on the highest parts of their raised designs. The designs on chased silver may have lost their sharpness, while engraved monograms or crests have often practically disappeared.

The fault lies mainly in the types of cleaner once used extensively by our ancestors. Most early home-made recipes called for abrasive substances such as jeweller's rouge or even brick dust. Proprietry brands of silver cleaner also contained these harmful substances, the gritty particles scouring the metal quite deeply. At best this resulted in a multitude of microscopic scratches which dulled the surface. At worst, combined with zealous and frequent cleaning the hallmarks might well fade away into obscurity. Once the punches have been eroded in this way, nothing can bring them back permanently.

Modern foam, liquid and cream cleaners are usually much less harmful to silver, although some of the latter still contain a certain amount of abrasive material. If in any doubt, place a small drop of the product onto the thumb and then rub it with the forefinger. Any sensation of grittiness must eliminate the cleaner, if you want to avoid the problems outlined above. If you decide to use a cream cleaner, then great care must be taken to protect the hallmarks. A small piece of clear adhesive tape or a thumb placed over the marks will be sufficient. The foam and liquid products are particularly useful for dealing with elaborately-pierced or embossed pieces, which can be attacked gently with an old, soft toothbrush. Small pieces can be suspended in the clear liquid for a few minutes, this ensuring that the cleaning fluid penetrates all the intricate nooks and crannies.

14 *Left:* the effects of over-zealous cleaning. Here the hallmarks have been practically obliterated on the blade of an Edwardian crumb scoop.

15 *Right:* a once attractive Art Nouveau hand mirror, Chester, 1905, now ruined by too much cleaning. The thin silver skin has split where the crest was engraved, and there are numerous little holes on the high points of the stamping.

After cleaning the pieces should be washed in warm, soapy water and then rinsed in clean water. This is very important, as the cleaner will continue to eat into the metal if not rinsed away. Items filled with pitch should never be immersed in water however, as this may cause the pitch to expand inside the hollow silver casing. Knives, dressing table pieces, and some candlesticks must be treated with great care. Their silver casings should be rinsed as quickly as possible in cold running water, to avoid this problem. While some modern products will also clean silver-gilt it can simply be washed in warm soapy water and then rinsed; a final polishing with a soft cloth will restore the warm shine. Steel knife blades must be dried immediately as they are very prone to rust. If they have already been affected, then they can be cleaned by rubbing gently with a damp cork dipped into a household scouring powder. This will remove the rust and restore some of the original shine, sharpening the blade at the same time.

Once the grime and tarnish have been removed, there are several ways of maintaining the desired shine. Regular washing in soapy water will remove slight tarnish, and in fact pieces in regular use such as cutlery should require no other form of cleaning. Dishwashers should be avoided, and it is better to wash each piece individually, thus avoiding the risk of damage as the various items scratch each other underneath the water. Once washed, each piece should be dried gently with a special 'long term silver cloth' impregnated with a chemical which will maintain the brilliant lustre. These cloths are useful for regular cleaning, each piece requiring a few seconds of gentle rubbing rather than a thorough and potentially harmful overhaul. It is better to clean silver little and often, than to leave it until drastic measures are called for.

Tarnish, an unsightly layer of silver sulphide, is caused by the metal reacting with sulphur present in many foodstuffs and even in the air which we breath. Eggs, fish, lemon juice, and vinegar react particularly badly, hence the frequent gilding of specific items of flatware likely to come into contact with these substances. Fumes from open fires and central heating, and cigarette smoke are also among the chief culprits, and it is therefore advisable to display silver behind glass rather than on open shelves. While it is delightful to handle old silver, even this can leave unsightly blemishes. Many museum curators use soft, white cotton gloves when examining their collections, and some shops also insist on this precaution, each potential customer being asked to don a pair before handling the stock. Although this is necessary when handling pieces of great antiquity and value, the majority of collectors have little need to worry about their friends picking up and admiring their prized possessions.

Display silver can be professionally lacquered, although this can mask both colour and brilliance. It is also only useful for pieces such as candlesticks or centrepieces, which simply stand untouched. Pieces which are used must not be lacquered, as the lacquer chips very easily. Once its air-tight surface is broken, then tarnish begins to creep underneath, giving an unsightly crackled effect. Damaged lacquer can be removed with acetone, but this is an unpleasant and dangerous task, better left to a professional. Black spots caused by fruit acids or salt are a more serious problem. They have to be buffed out by an expert, the process requiring the removal of a thin layer of silver.

Today there is a new chemical product which plates base metal, creating a thin, sparkling surface. While useful for restoring worn electro-plate or for brightening up badly tarnished pieces, it can also be used to disguise damage. I have already seen several pieces of silver with let-in patches, the solder lines concealed quite effectively in this way.

Some people may prefer to store their collection away from sight. If this is the case, then the pieces should be wrapped in sulphur-free tissue paper, readily available from both jewellers and milliners. Other wrapping materials can actually cause tarnish, because of the sulphur which they contain. Newspaper is particularly offensive, and I have often seen pieces which appear to be etched with newsprint, the acid in the ink having eaten into the metal. Rubber bands are also very harmful, the sulphur in the rubber reacting with the silver to leave black 'burn' marks. These are difficult to remove, requiring machine-polishing which may damage the piece itself. Once wrapped in tissue, the items can be stored in plastic bags. Alternatively, 'tarnish-proof' cloth bags can be bought from reliable suppliers. Some are more effective than others, and it is worth seeking advice from a silver dealer before investing in expensive, but possibly useless bags.

Salt is particularly harmful to silver, pitting and corroding the metal. Ideally, the interiors of both salt cellars and their spoon bowls should be gilt, although glass liners can do much to prevent salt damage. These are still readily available from specialist suppliers, who can normally fit a replacement liner from stock. If your salt cellars are an unusual shape, then it may be necessary for the glass manufacturer to make a special moulding. Obviously this will be more expensive, but still worthwhile if you wish to use your pieces for their original function. If special liners do have to be made, then it is worth ordering a couple of extras in case of breakages.

Small pieces of silver are quite difficult to display effectively, and many collectors despair, sometimes locking their possessions away into drawers or storing the whole lot in a bank vault. There are several ways around this perennial problem. Firstly, I am a great believer in using antiques, either for their original purposes or for a variety of new functions. The dining-table can be decorated with bonbon dishes and vases, and wine can still be strained through Georgian funnels. Buttons and buckles can turn a simple outfit into something exclusive and special. Odd eighteenth-century teaspoons are ideal for sugar and honey, and snuff boxes can be used to hold saccharins or pills. A group of miscellaneous objects arranged on a low table can be very pleasing, particularly if displayed beneath a lamp. Friends will enjoy picking up and handling such items, and the more unusual pieces will provoke much interest and conversation.

The Victorians delighted in displaying a multitude of gewgaws on corner 'whatnots' or on small sets of shelves. While pieces of nineteenth-century furniture are now expensive, there are many excellent reproductions available. Alternatively, one could use a turn-of-the-century folding sandwich- or cake-stand. Usually made from mahogany or oak, these dainty objects cost £50-£80 each, and their circular plates are ideal for displaying half a dozen silver objects. Old shop display cases are also perfect, and can sometimes be found relatively cheaply. Whether from a haberdashers, a tobacconists, or a sweetshop, these often contain little compartments which can be lined with coloured velvet, to create a splendid contrast with the brilliance of the silver. Small chests of drawers are also available, often beautifully made and veneered in mahogany or rosewood. These were originally used to house collections of birds' eggs and mineral specimens, and many have divided drawers with detachable glass lids helping to prevent the formation of tarnish.

Tiny objects such as thimbles can be displayed very effectively under glass domes. Victorian examples can still be found, sometimes filled with moth-eaten stuffed birds or melted and discoloured wax fruit. Brand-new domes are also now available, complete with sets of graduated shelves. Racks once used to contain printers' type can be adapted quite easily to form wall shelves, their divisions making neat compartments ideal for 'toys' such as vinaigrettes or snuff boxes.

Flat objects such as button hooks and shoe horns can be displayed in deep frames lined with richly-coloured velvet. Each piece can be sewn onto the background material. Splendid shell or fan shapes and extravagant swirls can be created in this way. I have even seen button hooks displayed directly against a dark wall, each one hung from a tiny nail. While this method allows for changes in design, one must be prepared to put up with several hours of cleaning each week. Alternatively, flat pieces look very attractive when arranged beneath the glass of a coffee table. Easily removed for cleaning, and yet protected by the glass, this can be an excellent way to organize a collection of fragile pieces.

Although cut-glass scent and cologne bottles are attractive in their

16 *Left:* This charming mid Victorian mahogany cabinet, the drawers enclosed by locking doors with Gothic panels, is only 20 inches tall. It would now make an ideal display case for small pieces of silver such as vinaigrettes or snuff boxes. Well-made, small Victorian furniture is now very expensive, and this piece would probably cost £800-£1,000. Cheaper versions in pine are still readily available however.

17 *Right:* old shop fittings make perfect display cases for small objects, protecting fragile pieces from damage and tarnish. This piece, made of stained oak, revolves to show off its contents. It probably came originally from a pharmacy or a tobacconists, and was made *circa* 1920. Today one could buy a similar piece for £150-£200.

own right, they can look even better if filled with brightly-coloured water and then placed on a window ledge. The sunlight shines through, creating an almost magical effect which will brighten up any room, as the various facets sparkle and shimmer to create a rainbow of beautiful colours.

Finally, it is a sad fact of life that anything of value is at risk today. One should therefore always make sure that a collection of silver is properly insured. Many auction houses and antique dealers will value for insurance purposes, listing each item separately with its current value and a brief description. Identifying features such as crests and inscriptions should always be noted, and it is worth photographing the more valuable items. Any extra information will help the police to track down your missing possessions, and it is well worth taking the trouble to make a note of new purchases with their prices. Insurance valuations should be up-dated at least every five years. Although the initial charge for a valuation may be quite high, most firms will do up-dates for a small amount of money, adding new pieces and adjusting the values to current market replacement prices. Despite the sometimes frightening insurance premiums demanded in today's high risk society, the expense is justified. It seems a small price to pay for both peace of mind, and the knowledge that one would be amply compensated and could start to collect again, if one should have the misfortune to be the victim of theft.

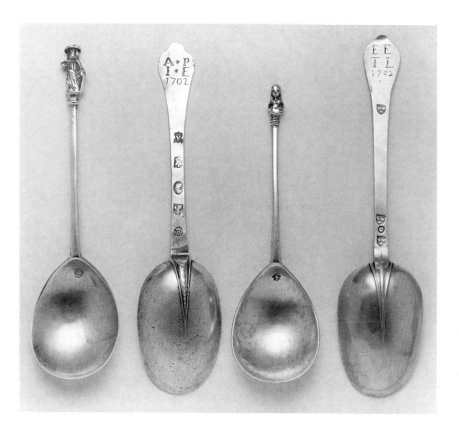

18 Four early spoons: *left* to *right:* Elizabeth I apostle, possibly St. Peter, William Cawdell, London, 1599, £1,000-£1,200; William III dog-nose, Richard Willcocks, Exeter, 1707, £400-£500; Elizabeth I 'maiden head', possibly based on The Virgin Mary, *c.* 1560, £1,500-£2,000; William and Mary dog-nose, provincial, *c.* 1690, £250-£350.

19 Six from a rare set of twelve Charles II trefid-end forks, John King, London, 1683. £10,000-£12,000. A single example would cost £800-£1,000.

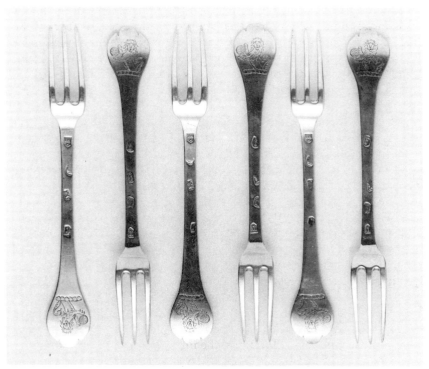

2 Cutlery

Cutlery

Cutlery can be divided into items used for everyday eating, and those with a more specific function, such as serving soup or fish, or measuring tea. Serving implements have become 'collectors' items', with a premium placed on their charm and rarity. The many kinds of 'collectable' cutlery are described in some detail later in this chapter, but first one must consider the development of table silver from the days when every wealthy person had his own individual set of cutlery, carried when travelling and even taken along to social functions, the host not expected to provide eating implements for his guests.

Until the mid seventeenth century spoons were personal possessions, given as christening or betrothal gifts. Most had fig-shaped bowls and straight, slender handles, often applied with a cast decorative finial. Today spoons with baluster finials or 'apostle' finials seem to be the most common, the latter with representations of Christ or one of his disciples. Although not particularly rare, it is difficult to find these spoons in good condition, and fine examples have become very expensive.

The Restoration of the monarchy in 1660 introduced many new fashions to Britain, Charles II having spent his years of exile as a guest of the French court. New styles in costume, furniture, and, of course, silver swept in from the continent, and the rest of the court followed the examples set by the king and his immediate retinue.

One important change was the introduction of table and dessert forks. Primitive combination forks and spoons called 'suckett spoons' had been in use for many years in Britain for eating crystalized fruits and preserved ginger, but most people used only spoons and knives. The first true table fork which survives, a simple but sturdy two-pronged piece of silver, was hallmarked in London in 1632, but this example is unusual. The introduction of forks was resisted by the more conservative people, who viewed the new implement as an eccentric and even effeminate whim. Others felt that forks were ugly and clumsy, or even dangerous. Despite these objections, the influence of the court gradually covered the rest of Britain, although isolated pockets of Scotland resisted

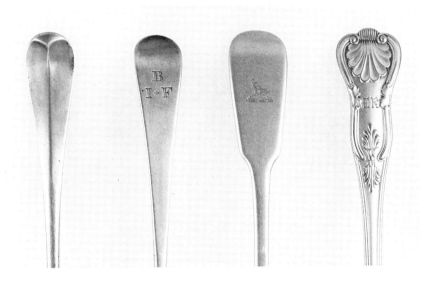

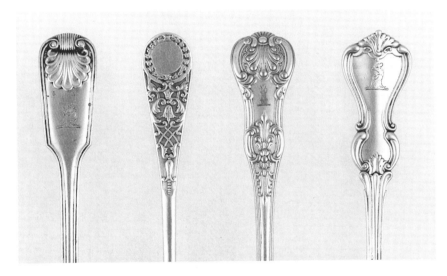

20 *Left:* the four most common flatware patterns: *left* to *right:* Hanoverian: Maker indistinct, London, 1738; Old English: Richard Crossley, London, 1781; Fiddle: William Bateman, London, 1837; Kings: George Adams, London, 1868.

21 *Below left:* four flatware patterns which are more unusual: *left* to *right:* Fiddle, thread and shell: William Eley, London, 1838; Venetian or Italian: Martin Hall and Co., Sheffield, 1874; Queens: George Adams, London, 1849; Albert: George Adams, London, 1855.

22 Occasionally one may find unusual pieces of flatware like these moustache spoons, the shaped 'ledge' designed to protect splendid Victorian moustachios when eating soup. The above were both made by Walker and Hall of Sheffield, one in 1892, the other in 1895. £80-£100 each. The cockerel egg scissors, used to cut the top off a hard-boiled egg, are made of gilt steel with paste 'ruby' eyes. £30-£40.

as late as the early nineteenth century. Forks were now made to match spoons, and table services on a vast scale were in demand.

This new fashion was helped by the introduction of a new design of cutlery with flatter, broader handles replacing the slender handles with cast terminals. This cutlery was ideal for the display of chased or stamped rococo scroll decoration, again inspired by French designs, and was also cheaper to produce, because the pieces were cut from hand-forged and hammered sheet silver requiring less assembly and joining. Sets of matching pieces could now be manufactured quite easily.

Today it is difficult to find complete 'straight' sets of cutlery, each piece made by the same maker in a certain year. Sets were frequently divided upon the death of the owner, each heir receiving a smaller incomplete set. Others were broken up, individual pieces auctioned or even melted down for their silver content, when entertaining on a mas-

23 Complete services are now very expensive, particularly if they are in a canteen. This set, made by Henry Harrison, Sheffield, 1895, contains twelve complete place settings along with many serving implements and several 'extras' such as a pair of knife rests and a pair of apostle fruit spoons. A reproduction of eighteenth-century styles, with Hanoverian pattern flatware and pistol-handled knives, it sold at auction for £4,200 in 1982. £10,000-£12,000.

24 Fish knives and forks were introduced towards the end of the nineteenth century. This set of twelve Queens pattern pairs is of particularly good quality, and the blades are finely-engraved with several different types of fish. Francis Higgins, London, 1876, £1,500-£2,000.

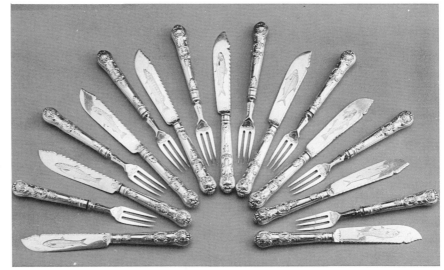

sive scale became too expensive for all but the very rich in the late nine-teenth century. As a result, an early eighteenth-century set would cost many thousands of pounds, with Victorian canteens often priced at £10,000-£15,000.

The collector of limited means should not be discouraged by this, but rather encouraged to try and assemble his own canteen, scouring the antique shops, markets and auction houses and perhaps paying very little over the current scrap price of silver to purchase odd pieces which can be matched. There are, however, several disadvantages to this method, not least the restriction of choice to the more commonly available designs. Hanoverian, Old English, Fiddle and King's patterns would all be suitable as they can be found with comparative ease. These patterns were first introduced around 1710, 1760, 1770 and 1810 respectively, but each has been in almost constant production, providing the modern collector with a seemingly unending source of attractive and useful pieces.

A further drawback is that antique and even second-hand cutlery will often be engraved with the crests or initials of former owners. Engravings can be erased by a good silversmith who could then add your own monogram or initials, but this would increase the cost of the set of silver by a quite considerable margin.

While patterns and sizes can be matched quite easily, it is far more difficult to collect pieces made by any one silversmith. If one adds to this the wish to acquire items bearing the same date letter punch, then the task seems almost impossible. However, a canteen of cutlery made by a single maker in any one year will always be more valuable than a mixed canteen, even if assembled at a later date, and it is less difficult to achieve this ideal than one might imagine. In the late eighteenth and early nineteenth centuries the manufacturing of cutlery was dominated by the Eley, Fearn, Chawner and Smith families, either individually or in

25 Two from a set of twelve table knives, the handles stamped from thin sheet silver filled with pitch. British examples are still quite common, although perfect specimens have become difficult to find. The above were made by Andrew Ellicott Warner, Baltimore, *c*. 1835. Despite their later replacement blades they are very rare. £6,000-£8,000.

26 Sets of flatware in fitted, plush-lined cases were popular wedding presents, although few seem to have been used, judging from the number still to be found in excellent condition. Francis Higgins, London, 1893, £200-£250.

partnership. Later in the nineteenth century Francis Higgins and George Adams were both prolific makers. The sensible collector should try to acquire pieces by the above makers, buying and selling to weed out poor specimens.

Most antique sets of cutlery should contain tablespoons, table forks, dessert spoons, dessert forks and teaspoons, but once these basics have been found the list of extras is almost endless. Both soup spoons with circular bowls, and fish knives and forks date from the second half of the nineteenth century. Similarly, grapefruit spoons, ice-cream spoons, oyster forks and pastry forks are all comparatively late inventions which may well have been commissioned to match and enhance an earlier canteen.

So far we have dealt purely with 'flatware': spoons, forks and other items made from flat sheet silver. Knife handles were made by the 'hollow workers', specialist silversmiths who bought the steel blades, attaching their shafts to the hollow handles by embedding them into molten pitch. This was allowed to cool and harden forming a tight bond. Better quality knives had cast handles, but by the mid eighteenth century most examples had handles stamped out from thin sheet silver in two halves, soldered together to form the reservoir for the pitch. One can rarely find early knives in good condition, and most people settle for bone or ivory-handled knives with steel blades. These are still quite inexpensive, and a set might cost as little as £10-£15.

Dessert Sets and Accessories

Although dessert spoons and forks were made *en suite* with larger pieces of cutlery from the mid seventeenth century, separate sets came into use in the late 1700s, often in their own individually fitted box. Most of these sets bore little relation to the plainer flatware used for the early part of each meal, and were often far more ornate, with engraved fruit and flowers and splendid gilding. Until the 1820s most sets contained only knives and forks for eating cheese and fruit, but as the nineteenth century progressed, dessert services became increasingly ostentatious.

In the nineteenth century it became fashionable to clear the dining table after the main courses of each meal, the servants removing all the cutlery and replacing it with a different set. Mrs Florence Hope wrote, in her guide to etiquette *Social Customs* (1887): 'for the dessert, a silver dessert knife and fork and a gold or silver dessert spoon are put at each place. To these is often added an ice-spoon . . .'. This new custom encouraged the introduction of new styles as the wealthy found an excuse to display their riches and sometimes rather dubious tastes, in their choice of highly ornate dessert silver.

In this period several ornate patterns such as Bacchanalian were created and used almost entirely for dessert pieces. Many Victorian dessert services survive and these are often in excellent condition, presumably protected by their wooden cases and used only on special occasions. Examples in mint condition, sometimes still wrapped in the original tissue paper, appear quite often on the market, presumably unwanted or duplicate wedding presents.

The most elaborate sets contained nut-crackers and picks, usually of silver-plated steel or nickel, as silver would be too soft for such strenuous duty. Many also had matching grape scissors, now much collected. Nineteenth-century grape scissors can be found in all the familiar patterns. The most elaborate were cast and chased with trailing vines and bunches of grapes, and are often awkward to use. Some pairs of grape scissors have steel blades to cut the tough stems, while others were made entirely of silver. Care must be taken with the latter in particular as they may become strained, failing to close properly, or

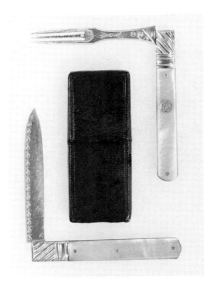

27 Although folding fruit knives can still be found for £20-£30, pairs of knives and forks are more unusual, retailing for £80-£100. The above set, incompletely marked but probably made in Sheffield or Birmingham, *c.* 1790-1810, have the added attraction of the original red leather slipcase lined in silk.

28 A Bacchanalian pattern sifting spoon by John and Henry Lias, London, 1879, in original fitted case. £150-£200.

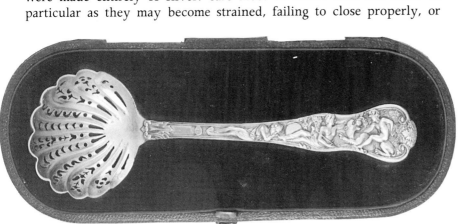

29 Selection of eighteenth- and nineteenth-century marrow scoops and two rarer marrow spoons, the latter London, 1718 and 1742. £80–£200 each. The presence of an original crest might enhance the value by thirty per cent.

weakened at the pivot, by the use of too much force. Cast specimens may have small cracks in their handles, which are difficult to repair, and the silver pivot screw may have been replaced with steel.

Large spoons for serving fruit compotes or sorbets were made to complement the smaller pieces. American examples are particularly ornate, with elaborate asymmetrical blades and bowls. Tiffany and Co. made many pieces based on Art Nouveau designs, with scrolling rococo decoration and finely-engraved monograms to match. A popular nineteenth-century idea was the conversion of plain tablespoons, often antique, into more ornate fruit spoons. Bowls were embossed with flowers and fruit, and handles were reshaped and chased with heavy rococo-style designs.

Apart from the dessert pieces made for table use, many items were made to be carried when travelling. The folding fruit knife must have been almost universal, judging from the number which still survive in good condition. Most examples were made in Sheffield, a well-established centre of the cutlery industry, or in Birmingham, the most important town in Britain for the manufacture of small novelty items, hence its sobriquet 'the toy-shop of Europe'. However, fruit knives were seldom fully hallmarked until the mid nineteenth century, with both date letters and town marks omitted more often than not. In the majority

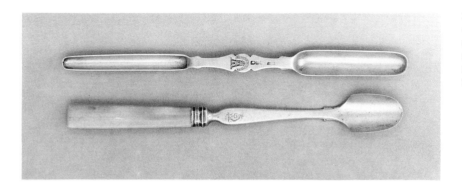

30 American marrow and stilton scoops closely resemble their British counterparts in shape and size. They are, however, much rarer, retailing for approximately ten times the price. These pieces were both made by Baldwin Gardiner, New York, *c.* 1830.

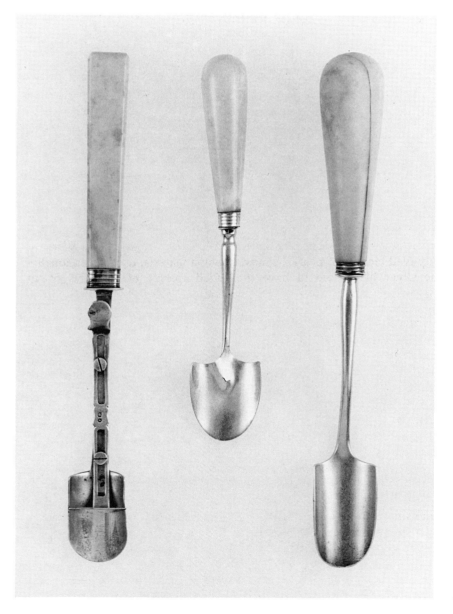

31 Stilton scoops, introduced in the late 1700s. These specimens were all made in London, *left* to *right:* 1834, 1792, and 1823, £200-£300.

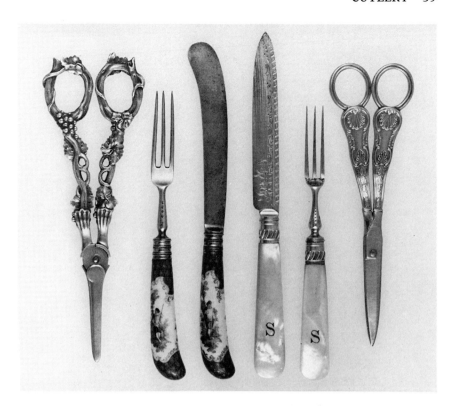

32 Selection of nineteenth-century dessert implements: *left* to *right:* Francis Higgins, London, 1867, £400-£600; George Adams, London, 1880, silver-gilt, £800-£1,000 a set; William Hutton and Sons Ltd., Sheffield, 1899, electro-plate, £200-£300 a set; William Eley and William Fearn, London, 1815, £400-£600.

33 Travelling apple corers were manufactured mainly in Birmingham, although the above example was made by Phipps and Robinson, London, 1796, £300-£500. Table apple corers are less collected. This was made by Aspreys of London, 1935, £70-£100.

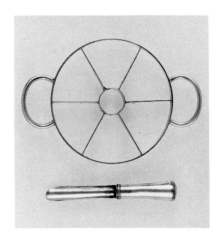

of late eighteenth- and early nineteenth-century folding fruit knives, the decoration was concentrated on the handle, with charmingly fluted or engraved mother-of-pearl the most common material used. Occasionally, the silver blades would have the added sparkle of some bright-cut engraving, but this was unusual, their thin gauge of silver perhaps causing problems for the engraver.

Folding fruit knives continued to be made well into the twentieth century, but later examples usually have steel blades, the handle now made of silver, often left quite plain or with simple engine-turned decoration. Sizes can vary, ranging from four to five inches for pocket or handbag examples, to less than two inches for specimens designed to hang from a watch fob, and all are delightful. It is well worth buying a knife in its original sleeve case, usually made of red leather. Occasionally, these knives are even accompanied by a small folding fork, for the particularly delicate eater.

Another dessert implement used by the traveller was the apple corer, its sharp, curved blade usually unscrewing to fit into a hollow bone or ivory handle when not in use. Examples in silver appear to date from the mid eighteenth century although the majority of silver apple corers were made in Birmingham and London in the nineteenth century.

Let us finally examine items created specifically for the savoury course, served after the pudding course in nineteenth- and early twentieth-century meals. Stilton scoops were introduced in the late 1700s, early examples often with straight blades and ivory handles. Some had

34 Flatware designed for dessert use was often more ornate than the pieces employed at the beginning of the meal. These are all American, manufactured in the late nineteenth century, and simply impressed 'Sterling'. £30-£50 each.

sliding mounts, or 'ejectors', to push the cheese onto the plate, simple mechanisms which are now often worn or repaired. By the 1830s, stilton scoops had become more sturdy, made of a heavier gauge silver, and they were often made to match services of tableware in all the standard patterns. It was quite easy for a silversmith to convert a tablespoon into a more collectable stilton scoop by simply reshaping the bowl, but such conversions give themselves away by their lack of weight. A genuine scoop should have a strong thick handle to withstand the pressure of turning the blade in the cheese.

Knives for serving hard cheese, with scimiter-shaped blades and silver-mounted handles, are relative newcomers, introduced in the early twentieth century. Some have been created using earlier handles, but the bright stainless steel blades soon reveal their modern manufacture.

A popular dish for the savoury course was marrow bone, segments roasted and served with salt and pepper. In the early 1700s implements with two elongated, curved bowls, usually of different sizes, were designed to facilitate the removal of the jelly. Marrow scoops were made from one piece of silver, and were always hallmarked on the narrow stem between the two bowls. This habit serves to make identification difficult, as the marks are cramped and even struck on top of each other to frustrate the collector. Early marrow scoops were small and sturdy, but they gradually became more elongated and elegant, the basic shape otherwise changing little until the nineteenth century, when they were made to match flatware services.

Most marrow scoops have both bowls facing the same way, but occasionally one can be found with bowls facing in opposite directions. Such specimens are rare and will sell for two or three times the price of ordinary examples. A further oddity is the marrow spoon, with one scoop combined with a bowl of tablespoon size. These date from the reign of Queen Anne and are often decorated with gilding and engraving. Sadly, many have been created from early spoons by reshaping the handles or, indeed, by removing them altogether, substituting a blade perhaps taken from a genuine but broken marrow scoop. These fakes are very difficult to recognize, as their makers would normally use gilding to conceal any tell-tale solder marks or joins.

Serving Implements

35 Five American turn-of-the-century silver-gilt serving pieces made by The Whiting Manufacturing Company, Newark, New Jersey, c. 1890-1905. The ivory handles are carved and stained to simulate coral. Such pieces would sell well today, particularly in the United States. £600-£800 the set.

36 Fine pair of fish servers applied with a crab and a fish. The blade and prongs are chased with a wave effect giving a distinctly Art Nouveau flavour. American, c. 1890, each impressed: 'Sterling' and with a capital C. £400-£600.

Soup and sauce ladles, and basting spoons were all made *en suite* with canteens of cutlery, but today it is more common to find them in isolation, separated from their original sets. Their appearance dates from the mid 1700s, and most followed the standard fashionable patterns of each period, with the progression from plain Hanoverian and Old English in the eighteenth century to the more elaborate designs of the Victorian era. An exception to this can be found in the 1740–1760 period, when soup ladles were decorated with rococo shell and scroll-work, or terminated in

37 This unusual fish slice and fork, the blade formed as a salmon, were made by Martin Hall and Co., Sheffield, 1882, £600-£800.

38 Nineteenth-century British and American slices were often decorated with fish and game birds, as illustrated here. *Left:* William Eley and William Fearn, London, 1822, £120-£160; *Right:* Hatden and Gregg, Charleston, Carolina, 1846-1852, £500-£700.

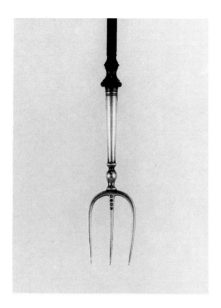

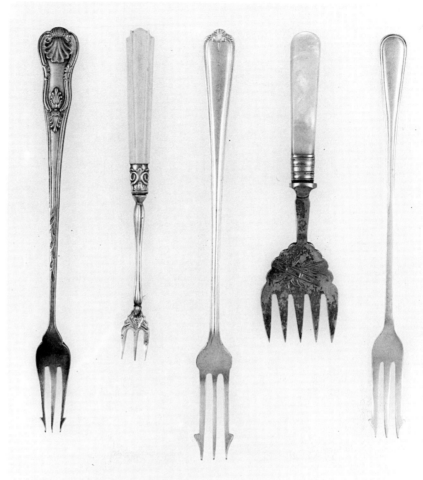

39 Selection of forks. *Above:* George III toasting fork by John Emes, 1798, £300-£400; *right:* four late-nineteenth-century pickle forks and a five-pronged bread fork, £30-£40 each.

a cast eagle's head, patterns which are not seen in flatware generally.

The bowls of soup and sauce ladles are usually oval or circular, but in the 1770s shell-fluting became popular, often in association with bright-cut or feather-edge engraving on the handle of the ladle. Ladles with shell bowls should be bought with caution as many will be split along one or more of the flutes. Plain ladles were often converted, their circular bowls fluted at a later date to make the piece more saleable. Such examples are generally too 'sharp', the fluting lacking the inevitable denting or smoothing down following many years of use.

Basting spoons were generally larger versions of tablespoons, although some examples were made with slender, pointed bowls and elongated narrow stems. These were used for stuffing fowls. Early eighteenth-century Hanoverian pattern specimens are among the biggest, and are commonly known as 'hash spoons' as it is thought they were used for ladling out stews made from left-over and reheated meat. A further early type of basting spoon had a hollow cannon-shaped handle similar to those found on some seventeenth- and eighteenth-century knives.

40 Selection of butter knives: *left* to *right:* George Adams, London, 1892, £30-£40; Mappin and Webb, Sheffield, 1912, £15-£20; Walker and Hall, Sheffield, 1902, £10-£15; Elkington and Co., Birmingham, 1908, £15-£20; Joseph Willmore, Birmingham, 1818, £80-£100.

An uncommon variety of the basting spoon is the straining spoon. This has a pierced divider running from the tip of the bowl to the start of the handle and was used for straining vegetables or lumpy sauces and gravies. Some were dual-purpose, with removeable strainers so that the spoons could also be used as ordinary basting spoons. The majority of straining spoons were made in Ireland and date from the late eighteenth century, although examples were made well into the Victorian era.

Trowels or slices were first made in the mid eighteenth century, and have triangular blades with fine saw-cut piercing, incorporating delicate rococo shell and scroll designs. Such slices were essentially dual-purpose, used for serving both fish and desserts. Although it is rare to find an example with a fish engraved onto or pierced into the blade, many had cast dolphin mounts joining the blade to the handle. The majority of trowels had turned ebony or ivory handles but some were of a basic Old English pattern, the handle terminal pierced with rococo decoration to match the blade. Early trowels can be difficult to date accurately as the hallmarks were often pierced by the maker, and consequently partially obliterated. They can however be compared with cake and fruit baskets with similar decoration, manufactured from the 1750s to the 1790s. Indeed, many were made by the same maker, William Plummer of London.

41 Asparagus tongs are now expensive if in good condition. *Top:* I.H., London, 1792, £600-£800; *Bottom:* William Eley and William Fearn, London, 1807, £400-£500.

The late eighteenth century saw the arrival of a new form of slice used almost exclusively for serving fish. Blades became rounded and handles were usually made in two halves stamped out from thin sheet silver and filled with pitch. The collector should not be deterred from buying pieces with different makers' marks on the blade and handle as many silversmiths bought ready-made handles from specialist manufacturers. The handle should, however, match the blade in date, any discrepancy indicating the replacement of a defective handle with one removed from another piece altogether.

In the early nineteenth century the fish slice changed again as the blade acquired a new scimitar shape. By now they were made from one piece of silver, the blade rolled more thinly than the handle, and were often an integral part of canteens of tableware, following all the contemporary patterns. The decoration degenerated to more simple designs, often with a rather stilted, mechanical appearance, and slat, star and roundel patterns became popular, produced cheaply using a fly-punch. With better quality pieces, the thin blade was often reinforced with an applied edge of gadrooning or scrolling foliage. This was cast separately and then soldered to the blade. For the first time, large forks made to match the slices became a standard addition, and engraved decoration began to assume a decidedly piscatorial motif, with fish amidst waterweeds, bulrushes and water birds such as herons and snipe obviously much in demand, judging from the number which still survive today. This thematic decoration reached its apogee in the Victorian era, with a variety of finely-engraved fishing vignettes including boats, nets and shrimp-girls.

42 George III pudding or fish slice, London, 1767, flanked by a Victorian fish slice and fork, Henry Harrison, Sheffield, 1880. The latter are better than most made in this period, with finely-carved ivory handles and bright-cut blade and prongs, hence £300-£400. The mid-eighteenth-century slice has been clumsily repaired with the application of a sheet of silver, a common feature which often spoils these items. £200-£250.

By the 1840s fish slices and forks were sold independently of canteens of cutlery, and were given their own fitted cases, usually made of leather and lined in silk and plush. Today a case in good condition will add some fifty per cent to the asking price. Plainer sets were made throughout the twentieth century, and are still in production today. These are in little demand from collectors.

Butter spades, miniature versions of the earliest slices, were made from the mid eighteenth century, and often have delicate turned ivory handles, sometimes with lovely green staining. These are rare, and perfect examples are now expensive. In the late eighteenth century butter spades were replaced by the butter knife with a scimitar-shaped blade, no longer pierced but often decorated with bright-cut engraving. Some were made with ivory or bone handles, while others were constructed from one piece of silver, the latter often made to match sets of tableware. Birmingham appears to have been the centre of their manufacture, producing particularly flimsy pieces with thin, fragile blades. Early butter knives were quite large, matching dessert spoons in length, but by the late nineteenth century they had shrunk to teaspoon size and had pointed, tapering blades.

The bread fork, a large two or three-pronged fork used to pass slices of bread at the tea table, is not unusual, but should not be confused with the toasting fork which is rarer. The former have relatively short handles, often made of silver or ivory, and flat prongs. Toasting forks have much longer handles, sometimes with a collapsible action for ease of storage, and deeply-curved prongs to hold the bread or muffin firmly during toasting before an open fire. Bread forks were sometimes sold with matching knives, the most attractive sets with spiral-fluted mother-of-pearl handles and engraved ears of corn on the blades and prongs.

Asparagus tongs closely followed the styles of sugar tongs, with andiron and scissor-action types and U-shaped examples all produced in the eighteenth and nineteenth centuries. Some had narrow blades, hardly useful for picking up cooked asparagus, and these are now generally called chop or steak tongs, suggesting a more practical use. All are popular and therefore expensive today. Unfortunately, as with sugar tongs, all asparagus tongs are prone to damage from the strain of over-use.

Tea, Coffee and Condiment Spoons

Few pieces of antique silver are readily available to the collector on a very limited budget, as even insignificant examples fall within the £50-£100 price range. Nevertheless, the collector can still find affordable Georgian and Victorian silver, if he specializes in small spoons. Tea and coffee spoons were made in all the standard flatware designs, although, like their larger counterparts, early examples are rare and expensive.

The collector is advised to start with Hanoverian pattern examples, first made in the early eighteenth century, their period of manufacture lasting some sixty years. Until the third quarter of the eighteenth century these small pieces made from thin sheet silver were incompletely marked, most bearing only maker's initials and a lion passant. In common with other flatware, the punches were stamped on the narrowest part of the stem near the bowl. When the Old English pattern was

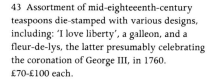

43 Assortment of mid-eighteeenth-century teaspoons die-stamped with various designs, including: 'I love liberty', a galleon, and a fleur-de-lys, the latter presumably celebrating the coronation of George III, in 1760. £70-£100 each.

introduced, in the late eighteenth century, the hallmarks were stamped onto the broadest part of the handle. Spoons were then fully marked, with plenty of space for the inclusion of town and duty marks and date letters. This more sensible method of marking has continued to the present day, although spoons with fancy terminals are often hallmarked on the back of their bowls.

The 'picture back' or 'fancy back' teaspoon is an uncommon variation, normally found in Hanoverian pattern examples or, more rarely, combined with Old English pattern handles. The undersides of the bowls are die-stamped with charming designs, often including rococo shells, scrolls and baskets of flowers. Occasionally this decoration is extended to include the end of the handle. Other examples can be found with pictures, some with political significance. Acorns and oak leaves, for example, refer back to the Boscobel Oak, the hiding place for Charles II in 1651, when fleeing from Cromwell's troops. These spoons were obviously popular with followers of the House of Stuart, and concealed their political message in a design which must have seemed totally innocent to all but a few *cognoscenti*.

Royal occasions were also celebrated, with crowns to commemorate the coronation of George III in 1761. Other designs symbolized peace and prosperity, sheaves of corn, hens with chicks, and milkmaids among the many images of economic stability and rural plenty. Perhaps the best-known of all picture back spoons are those made to celebrate the release from prison of John Wilkes, a popular writer and politician. He was arrested and imprisoned for daring to attack the government's foreign policies, but the populus rose to his defence, threatening riot and insurrection until the authorities backed down. On his release he made an impassioned speech to the assembled crowds, repeating the stirring

44 Today it is difficult to find a set of mid eighteenth-century teaspoons with sugar nips, still in their original shagreen (fish skin) case. Made by Stephen Adams, London, *c.* 1760, this set sold for £420 at auction in 1986, despite the moth damage to the silk lining of the box. £600-£800.

45 Souvenir spoons enhanced with American place names are much collected. This collection includes Fort Sumter by James Allan and Co., the Statue of Liberty by Charles Casper, and the pelican of New Orleans by M. Scooles. The others are unmarked or impressed: 'Sterling'. £10-£50 each.

phrase: 'I love liberty'. The teaspoons made to commemorate his victory depict an open bird cage, with a bird flying away beneath the celebrated refrain of Wilkes' speech.

All picture back spoons are unusual, even the most common shell or scroll designs costing as much as £30-£40 each. Any made to celebrate a particular historical event are even more expensive and the popular 'I love liberty' design is sometimes priced at £70-£100 per spoon. They were made from the 1740s to the 1780s, a fairly long period of manufacture, but are nonetheless quite rare. Thin gauge silver was used, an ideal material upon which the designs could be stamped cheaply and easily. The spoons could therefore be produced with the speed necessary to take advantage of current events and emotions. This lack of strength must have meant the loss of many examples, thus creating a ready market for perfect specimens today.

In the late eighteenth century and throughout the nineteenth century tea and coffee spoons became more sturdy, some Victorian examples weighing more than two ounces each. They were often made as part of a large canteen of cutlery, but frequently became separated from the rest, as they were not used in the dining room. Bright-cut specimens are especially collected, so the buyer must beware of plain examples which have been later-decorated. Genuine George III bright-cut Old English pattern tea or condiment spoons will show signs of wear.

From the mid nineteenth century, sets of tea and coffee spoons were sold in individual boxes, often accompanied by sugar tongs, sifting spoons and caddy spoons. Most of these sets were of poor quality, thin gauge silver, but one can often find them in perfect condition, their strong fitted cases having preserved them from damage. Many designs were available, among the most popular the 'apostle', the cast figure

46 Set of Art Deco coffee spoons, with black and red bakelite terminals, obviously designed to accompany games of bridge. Mappin Brothers, Sheffield, 1932, £100-£120.

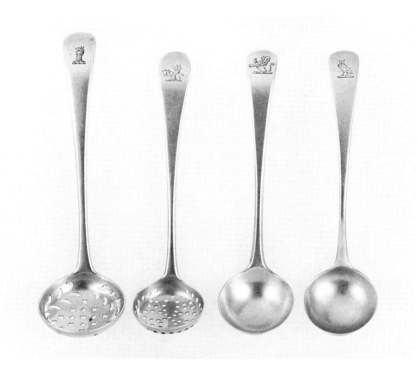

47 Four early nineteenth-century Old English pattern condiment spoons, each with original crest, the biggest only four and a half inches in length. Examples with pierced bowls are more difficult to find. They are thought to have been used for serving mint sauce. *Left to right:* Peter, Ann, and William Bateman, London, 1804, Richard Crossley, London, 1803; William Eley and William Fearn, London, 1806; W.C., London, 1820; £15-£30 each.

finial usually combined with a shell-fluted bowl. Every silver auction will contain several examples of cased Victorian and Edwardian tea and coffee spoons, and they are often inexpensive.

In the nineteenth century souvenir spoons were also popular, many with enamelled armorial terminals, or with bowls engraved or enamelled with views of holiday resorts, spa towns, or other places of interest. British examples are often rather dull. American and Canadian specimens on the other hand, are far more exciting, combining great skill of manufacture with vivid images and striking designs. Most were finely-chased with detailed decoration, making them much sought-after today. American souvenir spoons first appeared in the late 1880s, and were made by many different firms. They were very imaginative, commemorating not only places, but also events such as World fairs and elections, personalities, organisations, flowers and Red Indians. Very popular today, the Red Indians are especially sought-after, and one example depicting an Indian maiden in a canoe recently sold at auction for $600, an enormous price for such a small piece of silver of comparatively recent manufacture.

In the Art Nouveau period from the 1880s to about 1910, spoons and other silver were stamped or chased with swirling designs, often incorporating enamelling in 'natural' colours such as blue, green and brown. Many teaspoons were made by Liberty and Co. of Regent Street, London, with a deliberately unpolished and crude appearance, as if hand-made. Although this style was in keeping with current philosophies of design, because the Art Nouveau movement sought to alienate itself from Victorian mass production, Liberty's silver was actually made using modern techniques. Primitive-looking hammer marks were deliberately left to suggest laborious hand-beating, and ancient Celtic designs were adapted, creating a new range of silver-wares much copied by other makers. Despite this lack of true hand work, and the many poor adaptations of Liberty styles, Art Nouveau silver is very popular today.

Throughout the first half of the twentieth century sets of tea and coffee spoons continued to be made in large quantities. Art Deco guilloche enamelling in vivid colours and geometric designs is popular, as are spoons depicting animals, birds, and sporting motives such as crossed tennis racquets or golf clubs. Many spoons were sold individually, to clubs for competition prizes, with shooting and bowls perhaps the most readily available. Flower shows, dog shows, and even pigeon racing all had their own presentation spoons, although these are more unusual.

Like teaspoons, condiment spoons generally followed fashionable styles in flatware. The earliest examples had shovel-shaped bowls and Hanoverian pattern handles, and were large by today's standards, their length equalling that of a modern coffee spoon. Some unusual designs were made, whiplash handles were popular in the mid eighteenth century, and the Victorian era saw the introduction of many novelty patterns. These included the cayenne pepper spoon with cast devil's head finial, presumably to warn the inexperienced of the particularly hot nature of this spice! Once again, apostle spoons were popular. These were often sold together with curious salt cellars, the decoration of which was inspired by the Gothic revival of the mid nineteenth century.

Caddy Spoons

When tea was first introduced to Britain, in the early Restoration period, it arrived in wooden chests, usually packed around porcelain vessels which were often sold as receptacles for the leaf tea. The shapes of these vessels were soon copied and adapted by the silversmiths, who created small vase-shaped bottles and upright oblong boxes, each with a tightly-fitting detachable lid. This form of tea-container continued in use up to the middle of the eighteenth century, the lid used as a measure and also serving as a ladle to transfer the tea to the teapot.

By the 1760s tea caddies (the name derives from the Malayan word 'kati', a measurement of just over one pound), began to change. Fashion dictated the introduction of a box-shaped container with a flat or slightly-domed hinged lid, or a squatter, vase-shaped vessel with a detachable cover too large for measuring the tea. Thus in the mid eighteenth century it became necessary to introduce a separate spoon or ladle.

Early caddy spoons generally had a shell-shaped bowl. This is thought to stem from the inclusion in each wooden tea-chest of a real sea-shell, so that the prospective customer could sample the tea by smell and taste before purchase. The bowl, cast and then hand-chased, was sol-

1804 Geo III
B'HAM
Saml. Pemberton

1807 Geo III
LONDON
E. MORLEY

1811 Geo III
Birmingham
John Lawrence?

1811 Geo III
B'HAM
W. LEA & Co.

1811 Geo III
B'HAM
COCKS +
Bettridge

1812 Geo III
Edinburgh
MAKER UNTRACED

1817 Geo III
B'HAM
J. BETTRIDGE?

1818 Geo III
B'HAM
JOS. WILLMORE

1820 Geo IV
B'HAM.
MATTHEW
LINWOOD

1821 Geo IV
B'HAM.
J. BETTRIDGE

1832 Wm. IV
LONDON
JACOB WINTLE

1836 Wm. IV
B'HAM
GEO. UNITE

1840 VICT.
B'HAM
GEO. UNITE

1866 VICT.
Birmingham
GEORGE UNITE

dered to a scrolling handle with deeply-curved terminal so that the spoon could be hooked over the rim or handle of the caddy itself when not in use. Another variety made use of the traditional shape of the medicine spoon, a spoon with large bowl and short stem.

The more common use of the caddy spoon can be dated quite accurately as the 1777 price list of the Assay office does not include them. They are, however, mentioned in the 1790 Act as being liable for assay and hallmarking, despite their fragility. Caddy spoons from the end of the eighteenth century right up to the present day are still reasonably priced. One can speculate that hundreds of thousands were made as so many survive, often in remarkably good condition despite their appar-

48 Collection of nineteenth-century caddy spoons, no fewer than eleven of fourteen made by the Birmingham 'toy makers' who specialized in such small gewgaws. The earliest, *top left*, has a filigree panel inset into the bowl so that any dust in the tea would be removed, thus making the mote spoon redundant. The collection includes three caddy 'shovels', one with an ebony handle, another with a mother-of-pearl handle, and an unusual leaf-shaped specimen with wirework 'tendril' handle. £70-£200.

ent flimsiness. There are many different shapes of caddy spoon, the most common feature being the continued use of the shell-shaped bowl combined with variously-shaped handles, often enlivened with bright-cut engraving in the late eighteenth and early nineteenth centuries. This style was especially popular in the neo-classical period when shells were used to decorate all manner of things along with swags, paterae and rams' masks and hooves. Throughout the nineteenth and well into the twentieth centuries the shell maintained its popularity, perhaps abetted by the silversmiths who realized that the fluting served to strengthen the thin silver they often employed. Indeed, the pieces were generally called 'caddy shells' until the 1840s, when the term caddy spoon was introduced into popular usage.

Other popular and therefore mass-produced shapes included simple round or oval bowls, the acorn, the thistle, the leaf and the horse-hoof, all deeply-moulded to contain a decent measure of tea. One can also find specimens formed in the shape of a tiny shovel, with a turned wood or ivory handle.

Until the mid nineteenth century, caddy spoons were generally made of thin sheet silver, any 'chased' decoration die-stamped so that they could be produced quickly. As a result of this manufacture, skimped in both hand-work and material, many of the spoons found today will be in poor condition, their bowls splitting along one of the shell flutes or at the join with the handle. Some examples were cast and then hand-chased, and their quality is revealed by the heavier weight; others were made from one piece of silver, to eliminate the obvious point of weakness where the handle and the bowl were soldered together.

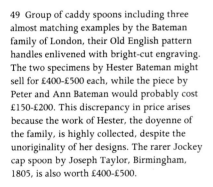

49 Group of caddy spoons including three almost matching examples by the Bateman family of London, their Old English pattern handles enlivened with bright-cut engraving. The two specimens by Hester Bateman might sell for £400-£500 each, while the piece by Peter and Ann Bateman would probably cost £150-£200. This discrepancy in price arises because the work of Hester, the doyenne of the family, is highly collected, despite the unoriginality of her designs. The rarer Jockey cap spoon by Joseph Taylor, Birmingham, 1805, is also worth £400-£500.

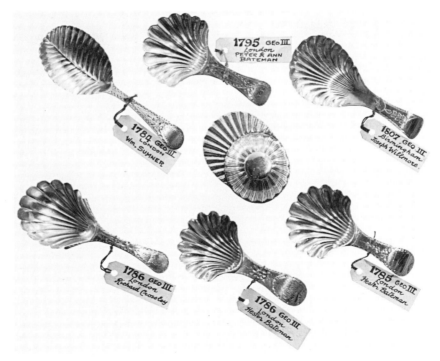

Caddy spoons can be found bearing the marks of all British towns of assay, although provincial examples are not common, with the exceptions of Sheffield, and especially Birmingham. The 'toy-makers' of this city produced even more caddy spoons than the silversmiths of London. Many of the Birmingham manufacturers gave their names to such pieces, although much of the work was actually carried out by small family businesses, each specializing in one stage of the manufacture such as rolling, stamping, engraving or polishing. London silversmiths usually used metal of a thicker gauge.

More modern caddy spoons frequently copy earlier styles, with the shell bowl still perhaps the most popular. Art Nouveau and Art Deco examples can rarely be found, although Omar Ramsden made some curiously heavy pieces with hammered bowls and Celtic-style knot and strap-work handles. Such pieces are popular today, their prices reflecting the current vogue for twentieth-century manufacture. Ironically, they now cost far more than the majority of their late eighteenth- and early nineteenth-century counterparts.

Mote Skimmers, Tea Strainers and Infusers

In the late seventeenth century and well into the eighteenth, imported tea was coarse and full of impurities such as pieces of stalk, dead insects and grit. The leaves themselves were roughly chopped, swelling when infused with boiling water and often blocking the narrow teapot spouts. To overcome these inconveniences the silversmiths invented a curious spoon called a mote skimmer, advertised in the London Gazette as early as 1697, and described as 'long or strainer tea spoons with narrow pointed handles'. It appears that these spoons, the bowls of which were decorated with piercing, had a dual purpose, being used to skim the surface of the tea to remove any debris, and also, perhaps, as caddy spoons, any dust falling through the holes being discarded. The wire handles were used to unblock the straight teapot spouts.

Mote skimmers generally bear only a maker's mark, often struck twice, with the occasional addition of a lion passant stamp. Despite this lack of information they can be dated with some degree of accuracy by close examination of the piercing and the handles. Late seventeenth-century examples have simply-pierced bowls and were constructed from two pieces of metal, their handles of uniform thickness and soldered onto the bowl with a rat-tail to strengthen the join.

By the early eighteenth century bowls and handles were made from one piece of silver, the handle tapering to a pointed finial. Although the piercing was still essentially simple, a few scrolls or quatrefoils began to appear by the 1720s. During the reign of George II, this piercing became far more elaborate, the hand-work rivaling that to be found on sugar castors and other larger pierced objects.

50 Two mid eighteenth-century mote spoons with hand-pierced bowls, each badly-marked but probably made in London c. 1760. £120-£160 each.

51 Two Dutch decorative tea strainers bearing import hallmarks for London 1896 and Chester 1898, and an Art Deco strainer with ivory button handle, by Catchpole and Williams, London, 1927, £60-£100 each.

52 This small tea strainer, made by G.R., London, 1823, is typical of the type developed in the late eighteenth century. Impractical and messy, few survive today. £120-£160.

By now the rat-tail had virtually disappeared, replaced by drops or die-struck patterns, often incorporated into the piercing. Throughout the eighteenth century the pointed finial grew longer, in some cases reaching almost half an inch, to cope with the massive tea-urns introduced for more formal occasions. Indeed, some very large mote skimmers can be found, matching in length the contemporary dessert spoon, although these are rare.

As mote skimmers are much collected they have, of course, been faked, a dishonest silversmith piercing the bowl of an eighteenth-century teaspoon and stretching and reshaping the handle into the required pointed shape. These altered specimens are usually out of proportion (the handles far shorter than those of genuine mote skimmers) and the piercing is often out of character for the period of the piece.

Tea strainers appear to be a comparatively recent introduction although fruit strainers were developed in the early eighteenth century so that the juice of oranges and lemons could be added to toddies with no risk of contamination from pips or pith. Some small tea strainers with circular, oval or lozenge-shaped bowls and wire hanging loops can be found. These were meant to hang beneath the teapot spout to catch the leaves. They must have been very impractical, drips of tea inevitably marking the polished table or table-cloth. The bowls were only about one and a half inches across, and needed emptying after one or two pourings. One can only assume that most tea-drinkers simply allowed the leaves to settle in their cups, emptying the dregs into the slop bowls which were a standard part of all porcelain and pottery teasets.

The tea strainer as we know it today seems to have appeared in the late nineteenth century, many ornate examples made in Holland and

53 A Victorian patent 'Teaette' infusing spoon with hinged cover, by G.G., London, 1893, pictured with an apostle sifting spoon by the Lias Brothers, London, 1879, a sugar spoon by the Lister Brothers, Newcastle, 1882, and a caddy spoon with shovel-shaped bowl and ivory handle by Joseph Taylor, Birmingham, 1812. £30-£70 each.

Germany and exported to Britain in large quantities. Many bear spurious 'antique' continental marks with the addition of a British import hall-mark, the latter dating manufacture to the period 1880-1920. Some are very decorative, with deeply-chased bowls incorporating rural scenes with milkmaids and contented-looking cows. Others are covered with flowers and fruit and have handles in the shape of mythical or historical figures, animals and even wind-mills with revolving sails. Often exaggerated in design, these tea strainers were decorative rather than functional.

In the early twentieth century tea strainers were normally smaller than their earlier counterparts, standing on little matching bowls designed to catch any drips of tea. Most were copies of eighteenth-century fruit strainers, with stands with cabriole legs and hoof feet, but others had slender ebony or ivory handles, or were decorated with Art Deco engine-turned zigzag decoration.

Today one can buy tea bags with little strings for making one cup of tea, but in the late nineteenth and early twentieth centuries tea infusers were used. These were normally egg-shaped, unscrewing in the middle, but occasional examples appear in the shape of tiny teapots. They have pierced bodies to allow the water to penetrate and removable lids for cleaning and replenishing. Always check the chain as some will have broken links. These may have been patched up with fuse wire and are not always easy to spot.

54 A Victorian egg-shaped tea infuser, made by Henry Meyer, London, 1892. Specimens with perfect chains can still be found for £30-£50, although novelty teapot-shaped examples are more expensive.

Sugar Tongs and Nips

From its introduction into Western society, tea was sweetened with sugar and by the end of the seventeenth century, British imports of sugar were estimated at around 70,000 tons, much of it brought in from the colony of Barbados. The bulk of this was used in cooking and preserving, or to sweeten the popular hot toddies and punches made from less palatable wines and spirits. Nevertheless much sugar must have been consumed during the fashionable tea-making ceremonies, the vogue for which swept across both Britain and America until even the poorer classes demanded their tea instead of ale or porter.

By the early 1700s covered sugar bowls and boxes were made as standard tea equipment, often in sets with teapots and caddies, and etiquette ensured the introduction of tongs to transfer the lumps of loaf sugar to the cup.

The earliest sugar tongs were based on andirons or fire tongs, with slender arms and curved ends, sometimes with a central spike running parallel to the arms for unblocking the teapot spout. The piece of silver

55 Three pairs of Victorian Harlequin sugar nips, two by the Goldsmiths and Silversmiths Company Ltd., the third by Francis Higgins, London, 1869, 1872, and 1879. They are illustrated with a pair of Art Nouveau enamelled fruit spoons by William Hutton and Sons, Birmingham 1908, and two from a set of six Art Nouveau enamelled coffee spoons by H.M., Birmingham, 1911.

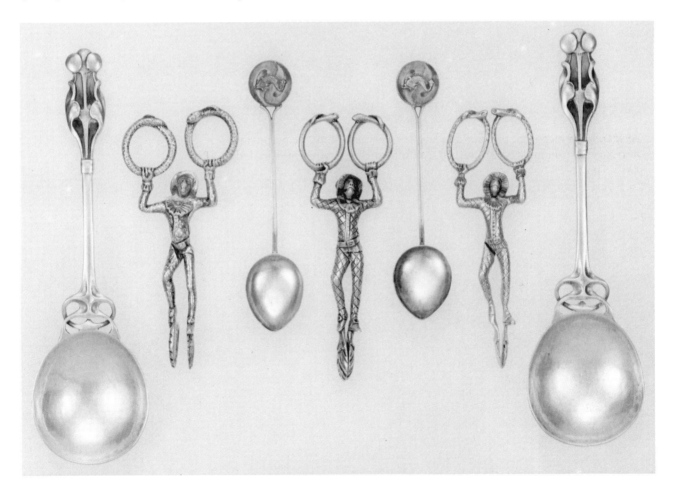

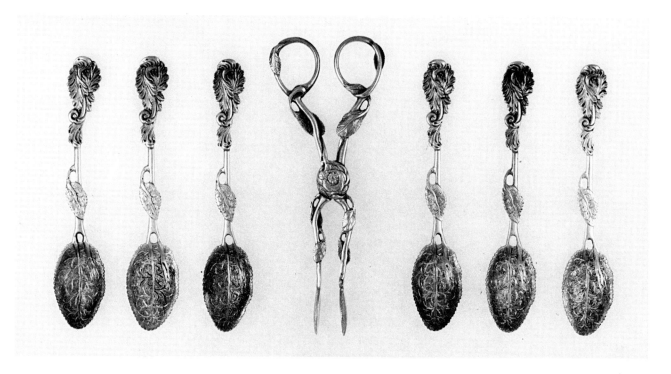

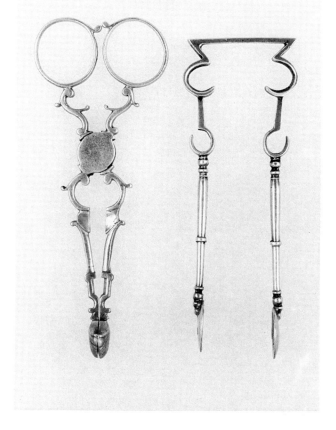

56 *Top:* rare set of unmarked mid eighteenth-century silver-gilt teaspoons and sugar nips decorated with rococo leaves. £600-£800.

57 *Above:* American nips and tongs closely resemble their British contemporaries. They are, however, much rarer, retailing for around ten times the price. The above was made by Jacob Hurt, Boston, between 1750 and 1758. They sold at auction in New York for just over $2,000, in 1985. £1,800-£2,200.

58 *Right:* two pairs of sugar nips, the scroll pattern example by Henry Plumpton, London, *c.* 1770, the 'andiron' type a Victorian copy of an early eighteenth-century style, by C. and Sons, London, 1899. £120-£180.

at the end was heated and hammered many times to give it sufficient 'spring' or tension. The earliest examples have small flat oval bowls but by the 1730s these were replaced by more practical dished bowls to grip the sugar, often decorated with rat-tails or die-stamped with flowers and foliage to match contemporary teaspoons. Few of these pieces have legible marks although makers' initials can sometimes be seen stamped inside the bowls.

The first scissor-action sugar nips with central pivots first appeared around 1715, again with rat-tail bowls. Often unmarked, such early examples can be distinguished by their straight baluster arms and plain oval finger loops. By the 1730s this sturdy design was influenced by the exuberance of the rococo, with delightful shell-shaped bowls or grips and elaborately-scrolling handles. This design continued up till the 1770s, the earlier examples again bearing makers' marks and often a lion passant stamp tucked inside the bowls, the later examples more fully hallmarked on the finger loops. Some even more elaborate sugar nips can be found, dating from the rococo period. These are cast overall with flowers and foliage and are usually of a much more solid construction. This variety was rarely hallmarked and consequently much reproduced in the nineteenth century, mostly in continental 800 standard silver. These later copies can generally be recognized without resorting to chemical analysis, as they lack the sharpness of detail in decoration executed with hand-chasing and finishing.

Although sugar nips were largely superseded by a revival in sugar tongs in the 1770s, novelty examples were made throughout the nineteenth century. Cast harlequin and ape nips can be found, and several years ago, Christies of South Kensington sold a pair in the shape of a 'Dutch' doll with enamelled head. A more common example of nine-

59 Selection of standard U-shaped sugar tongs, including an openwork example, London, 1771, and a bright-cut pair by Peter and Ann Bateman, London, 1795. £15-£60 each.

teenth-century whimsy can be found in wishbone sugar nips, perfect copies in silver of chicken wishbones, but sadly too flimsy for frequent use. All of the above novelty sugar nips are much collected and can realize much more than plain eighteenth century examples.

By the third quarter of the eighteenth century, sugar tongs had reappeared, these being cheaper to make than sugar nips. In the 1760s and 1770s they each had two cast and chased arms made separately and then soldered to the 'U'-shaped terminal, once again heated and hammered many times to give sufficient 'spring'. Many were crudely-pierced with rococo scrolls and shells or chased with stylized oak leaves, the latter examples usually with acorn-shaped bowls. This type of construction, using three separate pieces of silver was very fragile, and most of the tongs found today have been repaired, often with very little skill. By the 1780s sugar tongs were usually made from one piece of thin sheet silver and were now fully hallmarked inside the U-shaped terminal or along the arms. Unless by a popular maker such as Paul Storr, Hester Bateman or Paul Revere, they are quite inexpensive.

In the early part of the nineteenth century sugar tongs became much larger and heavier than their eighteenth-century counterparts. Being made of a much thicker gauge of silver, they seem clumsy in comparison. Some are so sturdy that they are quite difficult to manoeuver when picking up a small lump of sugar. A more practical alternative today would be a pair of late Victorian or Edwardian sugar tongs, which are usually much smaller as they were made to accompany coffee rather than teaspoons. These often have bird's claw ends instead of bowls, rather like miniature ice tongs, and are frequently enhanced with delicate piercing in the mid eighteenth-century taste.

Late eighteenth- and nineteenth-century sugar tongs can be found easily and cheaply, although sugar nips are more collected and expensive. Obviously, early specimens in good condition will always be at a premium, as will those made by the more celebrated and popular silversmiths. While American examples closely followed their British counterparts in both shape and decoration, they are much rarer, and retail for at least ten times as much.

60 Pair of Edwardian novelty 'Dutch' doll sugar nips by Carrington and Co., London, 1910. The legs are activated by squeezing the arms together. Sold at auction for £220, despite the damaged enamel head, this rare piece could now retail for £600 plus, once properly restored.

3 Further Dining-Room Silver

Condiments

Condiments and spices were an important part of the cuisine of our ancestors, their strong flavours helping to disguise the gamey taste of half-rotten meat and fish, and to enliven bland, over-cooked vegetables. Salt, in particular, played an almost mystical role, as it was commonly believed to be a symbol of piety, purity, and friendship. These qualities were reflected in the grandeur of early standing salts, finely-worked and often studded with jewels or adorned with enamelling. They were placed at the head of the table near the host and his more important guests, people of lesser rank were thereby reduced to sitting 'below the salt'. The value of salt in early times is reflected in another saying when we still talk of hard-working colleagues as being 'worth their salt'.

Although condiments made in the seventeenth century and earlier are rare and expensive, later examples are still comparatively common. As with most items, pairs and sets are particularly collected. There will also be a premium to pay for specimens made by celebrated silversmiths. Nevertheless, one could build up a collection of these small and attractive pieces without spending more than £150-£200 on each item. Condiments are useful to the modest collector as they display the complete spectrum of changes in style and the excellent workmanship normally associated with much larger and more expensive pieces of silver.

The commonest type of eighteenth-century salt cellar was the 'cauldron', a moulded circular vessel raised on three shell and pad or hoof feet. Quality varied enormously, and while most examples were light and delicate, some specimens were applied with cast swags and masks, the elaborate decoration sometimes concealing the basically simple shape. This design has maintained its popularity for many years, and there are many Victorian and later versions to be found. In the 1780s the shape was adapted by some silversmiths, who produced rarer oval cauldron salt cellars supported by four feet.

During the last quarter of the eighteenth century the cauldron shape was replaced by a more elegant vase shape, to reflect the current obsession with classical designs. The three or four fussy feet were now replaced by one pedestal foot, and many salt cellars also acquired scroll

handles and beaded rims. Bright-cut engraving also was introduced. Towards the end of the century this was often further enhanced with piercing, and the single pedestal foot was replaced by four stamped claw and ball or shell-fluted feet. Most cellars were now oval or boat-shaped and very light, their bodies made from thin sheet metal. Strength was added with 'Bristol blue' glass liners, the colour appearing through the piercing to create a most attractive impression.

Early nineteenth-century salt cellars were generally much heavier in design, fashions of the Regency period dictating the use of impressive table silver often enlivened with gilding. Shallow oblong trays on mask and paw feet were fitted with large cut-glass cellars supported by wire-work frames. The cauldron shape continued in manufacture, although increasingly elaborate decoration tended to mask the basic design. Both types of Regency salt cellar sell well today, and their prices reflect the quality of workmanship and the sheer weight of metal employed in their creation.

Casters for pepper, spices, and sugar originated in mid seventeenth-century France, the earliest design with tall cylindrical sides and 'bayo-net' fittings to lock the lid tightly onto the body. These 'lighthouse' casters were made in Britain from about 1670, with the first American example appearing in the early 1700s. Many were applied with cut-card decoration, and sets of three were often sold together for salt, pepper, and sugar. Gradually the bodies of casters began to swell until the full-

63 Pair of 'duck' salt cellars with spoons with 'feather' handles, imported into Britain by Berthold Muller in 1896, with import marks for London. £200-£250 the set.

64 While simple turn-of-the-century trefoil cruets can still be found quite easily, the above piece is a much rarer example of Victorian whimsy. Each condiment is enamelled in several colours, to simulate the egg of a wild bird. E.H.Stockwell, London, 1882, £700-£1,000.

65 Three eighteenth-century casters and an Edwardian reproduction. *Left* to *right:* London, 1767; London, 1747; London, 1775; Chester, 1908. Notice that the second example has been spoiled with later-chasing. This has resulted in the loss of the simple, elegant proportions of the two pieces on either side. £150-£300.

66 Pepper mills generally sell for £100-£150, although all silver specimens can bring a little more. *Left:* Stained or 'ebonized' beech and silver, by Elkington and Co., Birmingham, 1895; *right:* Cut-glass and silver, by Heath and Middleton, London, 1898.

67 *Below:* eighteenth-century American condiments are much rarer than their British counterparts. This delightfully simple kitchen pepper by William Simpkins of Boston, *c.* 1730, was sold for $4,200 in a 1985 New York auction. £3,000-£3,500.

68 *Above left:* these plain cauldron salt cellars could quite easily have been made in Georgian Britain. In fact, they were manufactured by Jacob Lansing of Albany, New York, in the second quarter of the eighteenth century. The pair might sell for £2,000-£3,000, compared with £300-£400 for a similar pair of British salts.

69 *Left:* three Victorian mustard pots decorated with machine-piercing, all made in London in 1855, 1843, and 1841. These small but useful objects are popular today. £250-£350 each.

blown baluster and pear shapes of the early eighteenth century were developed. Many specimens were of octagonal section, their bodies faceted to catch the light. Casters made prior to 1730 are often surprisingly heavy, with cast circular bases, applied body bands, and fine saw-cut piercing. Hallmarked underneath the foot or towards the top of the body just beneath the detachable cover, they are now very costly if in good condition.

By the mid eighteenth century most casters were much lighter, being made from rolled sheet metal. The baluster and pear shapes remained popular, but two other designs were also fashionable at this time. The 'bun pepperette' had a baluster-shaped body, but the steeply-domed pierced lid was replaced by a much smaller lid, usually with relatively simple piercing, reducing the overall height quite considerably to create an altogether squatter appearance. The 'kitchen pepperette' or 'dredger' also became popular, its simple circular box-shaped body applied with a sturdy scroll handle. The above styles of mid eighteenth-century casters are comparatively common, and it is still possible to find pretty examples in excellent condition.

Mustard was originally kept in casters which matched those described above. The lids not actually pierced but decorated with 'blind piercing', engraved shapes matching those cut out in standard casters. The earliest mustard pots were introduced at the beginning of the eighteenth century, but examples made prior to 1740 are now rare and expensive. Perhaps the most attractive type of mustard pot was the 'drum' variety. Most had flat or slightly domed hinged covers with pierced shell or cast scroll thumb-pieces, and scroll handles. This basic design continued in production for many years, often with the addition of stamped Gothic frieze decoration. Examples of all ages are now collected, if in good condition.

From the 1780s, vase-shaped pots on pedestal bases and part-fluted oval pots became fashionable. Made to match contemporary salt cellars,

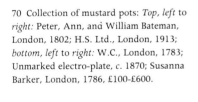

70 Collection of mustard pots: *Top, left to right:* Peter, Ann, and William Bateman, London, 1802; H.S. Ltd., London, 1913; *bottom, left to right:* W.C., London, 1783; Unmarked electro-plate, *c.* 1870; Susanna Barker, London, 1786, £100–£600.

71 Inexpensive condiment sets were made in large quantities at the beginning of this century. Today they are unpopular. Adey Brothers, Birmingham, 1932, £80-£120 the set.

they were generally fitted with blue glass liners and decorated with engraving. Plain oblong mustard pots were introduced in the early nineteenth century, their domed lids often applied with cast vase or ball-shaped finials. The scroll handle was largely replaced by the bracket handle at this time, and quality began to deteriorate.

In the Victorian era the Hennell family of London produced some particularly fine examples of novelty condiments formed as whimsical, but nonetheless realistic, animals and birds, including owls, monkeys, kittens, pigs, and even a kangaroo. These pieces now sell extremely well, often retailing for considerably more than their earlier counterparts. Lighter die-stamped novelty condiments are less expensive. Nevertheless they find a ready market, many collectors overlooking their stilted and mass-produced designs, because they are so charming.

During the late nineteenth century, fashion dictated that each place at the table should be supplied with individual condiments. As a result many sets of tiny and inexpensive pieces were manufactured. Today these small pieces are unpopular, although sets in cases can sell quite well if complete with spoons. Trefoil cruets fitted with salt, pepper, and mustard pots were also manufactured, each cruet rarely more than three inches in length. If complete these are more valuable.

Finally, silver-mounted capstan pepper-mills were introduced in the late nineteenth century, their bodies usually made of ivory, ebony, or cut-glass, although examples made entirely from silver can still be found. Specimens in working order are popular although, sadly, most now seem to be damaged.

Napkin Rings and Egg Cups

Although cloth napkins have been used in Britain since Roman times, the Victorians were the first to use them as table decorations, developing splendid ways of folding the starched damask to create wonderful flowers, pyramids, and fans. Used once for dinner parties, the slightly soiled napkins were then re-ironed and used again, this time by members of the family. Napkin rings to hold the rolled linen were introduced in the mid nineteenth century and were commonly sold in sets of four or six. The individual rings were often engraved with numbers to ensure that each person received his own napkin every morning. Silver napkin rings display a wide range of decoration. Many cheaper examples were simply engine-turned or die-stamped with arabesques, but some heavier specimens were hand-chased and even applied with gold initials.

Fortunately, napkin rings were popular christening presents, with the result that single specimens are still very common. It would be easy to build up a collection of different designs, including many novelty napkin rings, once manufactured in both Britain and America. Some particularly charming pieces are illustrated in a catalogue produced in 1886–7 by the Meriden Britannia Company in Meriden, Connecticut. No fewer than seven pages are devoted to napkin rings, the eighty-six different designs including many rings applied with cast animals, birds, flowers, and Kate-Greenaway-style children. Two rings are formed as chariots drawn by a pony and a goat, while the two most expensive at $33 per dozen incorporate specimen vases, a lovely idea for decorating a breakfast tray.

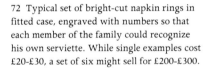

72 Typical set of bright-cut napkin rings in fitted case, engraved with numbers so that each member of the family could recognize his own serviette. While single examples cost £20-£30, a set of six might sell for £200-£300.

73 Two four-cup egg cruets by Martin Hall and Co., Sheffield, 1882, and Rebecca Emes and Edward Barnard, London, 1810. The 1810 example has contemporary spoons with ovoid bowls by Eley, Fearn, and Chawner, and is also fitted with a salt cellar. Today, the earlier would retail for £600-£800 and the later for £300-£400.

During the eighteenth and nineteenth centuries boiled eggs were often served in egg cruets, similar to condiment cruets in shape but fitted with four or more egg cups and spoons. Complete egg cruets are now very costly, but one can still find individual Georgian cups, the prettiest decorated with piercing, beading, and bright-cut engraving. By the early nineteenth century styles had become much heavier, with the introduction of gadrooning and fluting, some specimens weighing two or three ounces. Single egg cups were sold as christening presents from the 1850s, sometimes cased together with spoons and napkin rings. Once again novelty examples are particularly popular, one typical design with egg cup in the form of a broken egg shell, the base applied with a cast newly-hatched chick. Some twentieth-century egg cups were also shaped as caricatures of human bodies, the egg itself forming the head.

Egg spoons can be recognized by the shape of their bowls. Examples made before the 1850s commonly have elongated oval bowls, similar to but larger than those of contemporary mustard spoons. Most later specimens have horseshoe-shaped bowls. Normally inexpensive, a single egg spoon should cost very little, although sets of half a dozen are quite popular.

Bonbon Dishes and Specimen Vases

The pierced bonbon dish was introduced in the early eighteenth century, finding immediate popularity as a means of displaying and serving sweetmeats and nuts. Most were oval in shape, although this simple outline was often lost beneath a mass of cast and applied rococo shell and scroll decoration. Early examples often had two fixed handles,

one soldered at either end of the bowl, but by the 1740s the central handle came into use, usually pivoting for ease of carrying and storage. Raised from thick sheet silver and often surprisingly heavy, these pretty but sturdy baskets are highly prized. It was the custom to send them for assay and marking before the pierced designs were cut out using hand saws, and it is therefore quite common to find that the marks are partially obliterated.

By the 1760s cheaper, lighter bonbon dishes became fashionable. These were made from thin sheet silver produced by flattening the metal between heavy rollers. This inexpensive process replaced the time-consuming and laborious hand-raising necessary only a few years before. The pierced decoration was still cut by hand, and close inspection with a magnifying glass should reveal the jagged edges left by the teeth of the saw. At this time neo-classical motives such as vases, swags, and paterae made an appearance. Many examples were further enhanced with bright-cut engraving and applied beaded rims.

Many bonbon dishes made during this period were designed to hang from the branches of table centrepieces and, as a result, may well be incompletely marked. When submitted for assay they were treated as detachable componants of the centrepiece. Each basket was therefore stamped only with the lion passant and maker's mark punches. Such pieces will be worth rather less than their fully-marked counterparts.

The rise of the fused plate industry towards the end of the eighteenth century posed an enormous threat to the silversmiths, who were unable to compete with the flood of inexpensive wares pouring out from Sheffield and Birmingham. At first, piercing proved problematical for the manufacturers of fused plate, as the saw cuts revealed the tell-tale

74 Shell-shaped dishes were first made in the early eighteenth century, and were used for bonbons or for butter. These reproductions, both by David and Morris Davies, London, 1898, would now sell for £100-£150 each.

75 Inexpensive bonbon dishes with stamped decoration were produced in large quantities at the turn of the century. Often flimsy, single specimens are unpopular, selling for £30-£50. Pairs are more collected however, retailing for £100-£150. *Top:* William Comyns, London, 1894; O.Ltd., Birmingham, 1913; *bottom:* William Hutton and Sons Ltd., Sheffield, 1895; O.Ltd., Birmingham, 1915.

colour of copper. Resourceful and enterprising, they soon developed the fly-punch, a steam-driven machine which could stamp out innumerable designs using a hardened steel punch. At the same time the thin silver skin would be stretched through the hole, so disguising the much thicker layer of copper. Considerably cheaper than time-consuming hand sawing, this invention was soon adopted by the silversmiths who began to produce thousands of pretty baskets, sugar vases, and cream pails. The 1780s also saw the introduction of pieces made from drawn silver wire, often applied with cast swags and cartouches. The majority of these delightful items were fitted with 'Bristol blue' or ruby glass liners. Today these are often broken or missing after so many years of use. Fortunately, replacements can be obtained quite easily, although the colours of modern glass appear to lack the intensity and richness of that made in the eighteenth century.

During the nineteenth century dining habits changed with the introduction of *le diner à la Russe* from Europe. The various savoury courses were served one by one by the servants instead of being placed *en masse* at the centre of the table throughout the meal. Moreover, the old custom of removing the table cloth after the main courses became decidedly unfashionable. There was now plenty of room for a variety of decorative pieces of silver including sweetmeat dishes and vases, their colourful contents adorning the dining room for the entire evening and often containing the dessert.

Victorian baskets frequently reproduced earlier styles, and many fine copies are still available, sometimes retailing for almost as much as the originals they imitate. At the turn of the century however, quality began to deteriorate, and most bonbon dishes produced at this time suffered from the ill-effects of mass-production, with die-stamped floral and foliate decoration. The oval shape was still popular, but shell and

76 Three American late nineteenth- or early twentieth-century vases, *Left* to *right:* Samuel Kirk and Son, Baltimore, *c.* 1896, eight and a half inches; La Pierre Manufacturing Co., Newark, *c.* 1890, twelve and a half inches; Tiffany and Co., New York, *c.* 1915, twenty inches. The left-hand example is made from silver and patinated copper. It sold for $1,100 at auction in 1985. £200-£700.

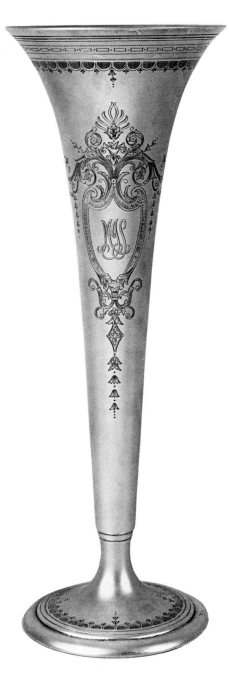

77 Four late nineteenth- and early twentieth-century British specimen vases, originally sold in pairs. Chased or stamped examples can sell quite well, but plain vases are in little demand, unless in perfect condition. £50-£150.

heart shapes were also manufactured in large quantities. Although quite attractive, these late specimens lack both weight and quality. While pairs or sets of four dishes are popular, individual specimens may cost very little, even if in good condition.

By the 1920s bonbon dishes were sometimes vaguely influenced by Art Deco designs. Angular, octagonal shapes, stepped ivory or bakelite handles, and engine-turned decoration remained popular until the 1950s. Antique pieces were still copied however, and earlier bonbon dishes provided the inspiration for flimsy adaptations of eighteenth century styles. Often stereotyped in design, and with simple stamped friezes of pierced slats and roundels, these items are in little demand today.

The use of silver vases and centrepieces became particularly widespread in the mid nineteenth century. While many were vast, each heavy silver or plated base supporting as many as a dozen cut, frosted, or coloured glass vases and bowls, more simple 'specimen vases' were also produced in large quantities. Designed to hold a single flower with a small spray of fern to decorate each place at the table, they created a charming setting particularly suitable for light suppers. The idea spread from the dining room into the bedroom and the parlour as the century progressed, and many thousands of these vases were produced in both Britain and America. The majority are between six and eight inches in height, with weighted bases to ensure stability. While most were decorated with spot-hammering or stamped with fluting and arabesques, some prettier examples were pierced with flowers, the latter type fitted with a blue glass liner to contain the water. Although specimen vases are quite common, it is unusual to find examples in good condition.

A Dining Room Miscellany

Throughout the last century and well into the early 1900s vast meals were the order of the day for the wealthy. Four or five distinct courses were normally served, and special occasions could easily warrant a dozen entrées and a choice of several desserts. Such elaborate banquets called for the creation of menu cards, often decorated with delicate watercolours or scraps of lace and dried flowers by the ladies of the house. A card would stand at each place, often supported by a silver or porcelain menu holder.

Although such elaborate meals became a thing of the past during World War I, when even the very rich found it increasingly difficult to maintain their vast armies of kitchen staff who were drawn to more lucrative factory work, the menu holder remained popular until the 1940s. Eventually, it was adapted to hold small cards inscribed with the names of the guests. This enabled the prudent hostess to plan her seating arrangements, avoiding possibly embarrassing situations and also ensuring that timid debutantes were surrounded by potential husbands.

Silver menu and place card holders are still readily available. Many incorporate family crests while others are more whimsical, with applied paste thistles, horseshoes, or tiny cast animals and birds. In the Edwardian era new designs were introduced. Oval tortoiseshell examples inlaid with paterae and swags became popular, as did menu holders finely-enamelled with gun dogs and game birds. Others were more simple, their plain circular discs allowing the owner to have his initials or arms

78 Two sets of menu holders in cases: *top:* William Hutton and Sons Ltd., Sheffield, 1922; *bottom:* Goldsmiths and Silversmiths Co. Ltd., London, 1908, £500-£600 each.

79 Menu holders: pierced with cherubs, S.B.and S., Birmingham, 1888; pierced with hunting scenes, S.G., London, 1894; eighteenth-century figures, Walker and Hall, Sheffield, 1918; Plain discs, Sampson Mordan and Co., London, 1931; Small scallop shell, Tiffany and Co., New York, *c.* 1920, £15-£50.

engraved for a small extra cost. This type is illustrated in the 1929 Harrods' catalogue, where a set of four small examples in a fitted velvet-lined case retailed for £2. 2s. 6d. Three other designs are also shown, the most expensive at 11s. 6d. each, with an amusing owl's face with 'boot-button' glass eyes.

Today menu holders are much collected, particularly if still in sets and with their original fitted cases. Those enamelled or applied with game birds seem to be the most popular. Tortoiseshell examples and those applied with comical owls are slightly cheaper, but even plain menu holders will sell quite well.

At the turn of the century some menu holders were modelled on photograph frames, with plain narrow silver mounts and easel supports.

80 Two pairs of knife rests, the dumbell pair by Walker and Hall, Sheffield, 1896; the silver and ivory pair by James Dixon and Sons, Sheffield, 1897. £100-£150.

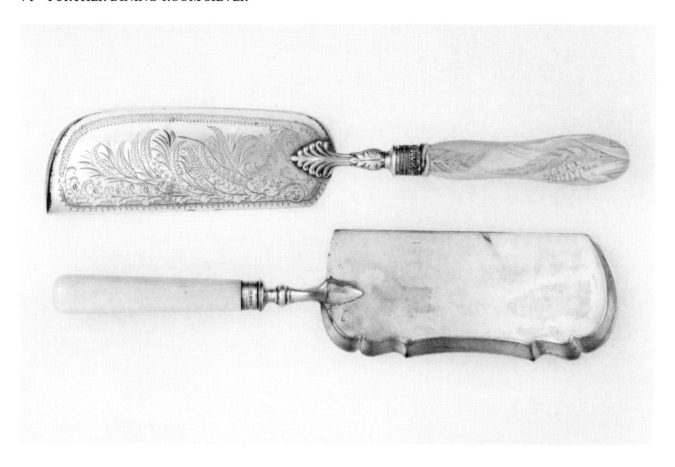

These were fitted with removable unglazed porcelain plaques, enabling each menu to be written and then erased, so the plaques could be used over and over again. Although more unusual than their smaller counterparts described above, these pieces are less popular. As a result many have been converted into photograph frames, by simply removing the porcelain plaque and inserting glass and velvet-covered wood, to create a more saleable object in today's market.

One piece of antique silver sometimes difficult to identify is the knife rest. These items were made in porcelain from the mid eighteenth century, and were sold in pairs. Their function was to act as rests for the carving knife and fork, so preventing grease from marking the polished table. Early silver examples dating from the 1780s and 1790s were similar in shape to their porcelain predecessors, being of triangular section and made from drawn wire. In the early nineteenth century this design was replaced by a single bar of silver supported on legs. The latter often took the form of an X, although grander examples were supported by cast dolphins or scrolling foliage. This design continued to be made well into the twentieth century. American knife rests are often more imaginative with supports cast in the shape of various animals such as pug dogs or bears. Although plated examples are quite common, American silver novelty knife rests are rare and much collected.

81 Two silver and ivory crumb scoops: *top:* Sheffield, 1877; *bottom:* Sheffield, 1913, £40-£100.

While circular silver-mounted glass teapot stands are still readily available, their thin silver mounts pierced and engraved with scrolling foliage, it has become quite difficult to find a set of six or more table mats. These pieces were made in large quantities from the late 1800s up to about 1940, and individual specimens are quite common.

Finally, after the savoury courses of each meal had been consumed, the table would be cleared and swept free of crumbs ready for the dessert and coffee. Crumb scoops were developed for this purpose in the late nineteenth century, each with a curved flat blade usually attached to an ivory or antler handle. These implements are relatively unsaleable today. As a result they are sometimes labelled as cake slices or egg servers, in the hope that the unwary collector may be fooled into parting with his money more easily. Crumb scoops required matching silver-mounted brushes, and a more sophisticated gadget which could be operated with one hand was developed in the early twentieth century. Based on the carpet sweeper in design and with revolving bristle brushes, examples are now very rare, even in silver plate. The *de-luxe* silver-mounted version is more difficult to find, and an example in working order would be popular today.

82 One of a set of six table mats six inches in diameter, made by the Goldsmiths and Silversmiths Co. Ltd., London, 1937, to commemorate the coronation of King Edward VIII. As the king was not actually crowned, renouncing the throne in favour of his younger brother, this set is rare. £600-£800.

4 Alcoholic Antiques

Punch and Toddy Apparatus

In the second half of the seventeenth century punch became very popular. The name of this concocted mixture is possibly derived from an Indian word meaning 'five', referring to the essential ingredients of wine, spirit (usually brandy), sugar, spices, and fruit juice. Recipes were jealously guarded by butlers and housewives, and the making and serving of punch, whether heated or chilled, became a ceremonial occasion calling for fine equipment, often supplied by the silversmith.

Punch ladles in several different styles are readily available to the collector for a relatively small outlay. Most of the early examples have handles made from turned fruitwood, *lignum vitae* or ivory, although the reign of George III saw the beginning of a vogue for silver-mounted whalebone. This was heated under pressure with steam until malleable and then twisted into ornate spirals, hardening and retaining the design upon cooling. Seventeenth- and early eighteenth-century ladles had bowls raised from hammered sheet silver of a heavy gauge. Although most were formed as deeply-moulded circles, oval specimens can also be found. A more unusual variety was the 'goose egg' ladle, named after the shape of its bowl.

In the second quarter of the eighteenth century ladle bowls were generally made from thinner silver, often fluted to add strength. Many were made from silver-mounted exotic materials such as cowrie shells or polished coconuts. The mounts are usually unmarked and therefore difficult to date. The 1740s saw the introduction of a new style of punch ladle, with the silver bowl formed as a nautilus shell. These were often plain but sometimes had delightful rococo chasing.

By the 1760s most punch ladles were flimsy and light, and their bowls were often made from hammered and raised crown pieces. Many had a gilt sixpence or shilling inset into the centre of the bowl, serving to strengthen the weakest part of the raising and sometimes helping to date the piece, although many silversmiths used Queen Anne or George I coins. This can, of course, confuse the collector, who may wish to ascribe an impossibly early date to such a piece. Few examples were hallmarked, although one can often see traces of lettering around the rim of the bowl.

This lettering remains from the design on the coin defaced by the silversmith.

In the late eighteenth century punch became unfashionable. Toddy, a stronger beverage made from sweetened and diluted spirits, became the more elegant drink to serve at social gatherings. As toddy was much more potent than punch, smaller ladles were developed, copying punch ladles in both shape and decoration. Many were made by the Scottish silversmiths of Edinburgh and Glasgow, and are often fully hallmarked in their bowls.

Although both Greek and Roman strainers have been found, these were usually made from base metals. The British silver fruit strainer made its appearance only in the mid seventeenth century. Most early examples have two flat, pierced handles applied to their deeply-moulded bowls, although some specimens have been found with single flat handles or with tapering tubular handles, similar to those on some contemporary soup ladles (see chapter 2). In the seventeenth and early eighteenth centuries strainer bowls were pierced with simple roundels, normally arranged in concentric circles but occasionally following more elaborate, over-lapping patterns.

As the eighteenth century progressed, the handles became more elaborate, with fine saw-cut rococo scrolling foliage and shells incorporated into their pierced decoration. By 1720 the bowls were often pierced with stylized flower shapes, and the better examples had intricate sawn designs similar to those found in mote spoons (see chapter 2). Many had a small clip soldered to one of the handles, so that the strainer could be attached to the rim of the punch bowl when not in use. As many eighteenth century strainers are so alike, it has been argued that they were probably made by a small group of London silversmiths who may not have registered their own marks at Goldsmiths' Hall. A more unusual type of late eighteenth-century strainer had large scrolling handles made

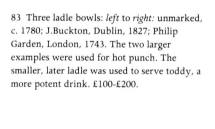

83 Three ladle bowls: *left* to *right:* unmarked, c. 1780; J.Buckton, Dublin, 1827; Philip Garden, London, 1743. The two larger examples were used for hot punch. The smaller, later ladle was used to serve toddy, a more potent drink. £100-£200.

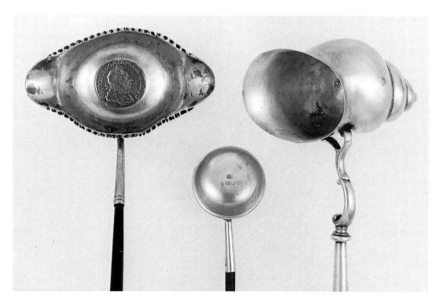

84 *Left:* Large 'butler's' grater by Rawlins and Sumner, London, 1842. These are now rare and much collected. £800-£1,000.

85 *Right:* George III table grater by Matthew Boulton, Birmingham, 1795. The steel grill fits inside a silver case when not in use. Boulton is better known for his larger pieces, made in both silver and fused plate, and it is now difficult to find small toys such as nutmeg graters or snuff boxes. £400-£500. *Photograph by courtesy of the Birmingham Assay Office.*

86 Five George III nutmeg graters, the largest two inches long. The top right example is decorated with bright-cut engraving typical of the period 1770-1790. This is still sharp after two centuries of use. £300-£500.

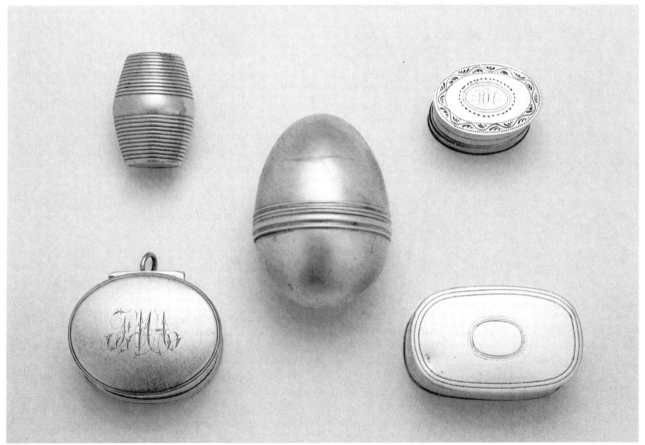

87 Two eighteenth-century fruit strainers, *left* to *right:*Benjamin Burt, Boston, c. 1755, £2,500-£3,000; London, 1739, £250-£300. American and British examples are very similar in form, although British strainers usually have more elaborate, hand-sawn piercing. Notice that the piercer has cut through the hallmarks of the London piece, obliterating the maker's mark and therefore reducing the value.

from gadrooned or beaded narrow strips of silver, which increased the overall length to as much as nine or ten inches. Although mid eighteenth-century fruit strainers are not rare, good examples with legible hallmarks are difficult to find.

Early spice boxes were usually tear-drop or heart-shaped. Some examples had scratch-engraved primitive flowers and contemporary initials. Constructed from thin sheet silver, their fragility has ensured that few have survived in good condition. Some spice boxes were fitted with steel grills for grating nutmeg, a spice introduced to Britain from the Indies and first valued as a protection against the plague. Its delicate, aromatic flavour soon became an integral part of most punch and toddy recipes, and by the beginning of the eighteenth century nutmeg graters were made in large quantities.

Most early specimens were formed as small boxes with provision to store the whole spice when not in use, and several shapes were popular, including the acorn and the cylinder. In the mid eighteenth century, many were embellished with delightful rococo shells and scrolls. By the 1760s new shapes had become fashionable, with egg, barrel, vase and boat-shaped nutmeg graters being amongst the most popular. Many were enlivened with bright-cut engraving, perhaps the most typical of all forms of decoration during the first twenty years of the reign of George III. Larger graters resembling modern cheese graters are very rare. These have exposed grills and D-shaped handles. They were designed to hang from a butler's belt with corkscrews, keys, and other pieces of equipment. Often as much as six inches in height, these graters now sell extremely well. A further rarity is the combination nutmeg grater and corkscrew, described later in this chapter.

Corkscrews and Bottle Openers

Corkscrews in all shapes and sizes have become much collected in recent years, on both sides of the Atlantic. Most are made from brass, wood, and bone combined with a steel or iron screw, because silver is too soft and malleable a metal to be used for the successful removal of well-embedded corks. However, silver was employed to fashion the handles and mounts of corkscrews.

Silver-cased and handled travelling corkscrews were made in large quantities throughout the eighteenth century. Many had a tapering cylindrical holder or sheath to conceal the sharp screw when not in use. This holder was often decorated with reeding or beading, and screwed onto the upper section of the shaft. In some cases, the screw would have a cross-bar or oval wirework handle, but many had a small loop attached to the end of the steel shaft. The cylindrical sheath could be inserted through this to create a T-shaped handle with excellent leverage. This type often incorporated a seal, deeply-engraved with initials or a crest and soldered to the upper part of the loop. This was presumably used to mark bottles after corking and sealing with molten wax.

Although these corkscrews were made from the late 1600s, early examples are scarce. The majority of specimens available to the modern collector were made in Birmingham in the last quarter of the eighteenth century. Many were incompletely hallmarked, bearing only makers' initials, usually stamped underneath the foot of the sheath.

Many sheath-type corkscrew cases were made entirely from silver, but others were manufactured from ivory, often inlaid with gold and silver piqué decoration or tightly-bound with silver wires. Some were engraved or inlaid with initials and dates, and rare examples are stained and engraved with perpetual calenders. Other sheath-type travelling corkscrews have mother-of-pearl, hardstone, or enamel T-shaped handles, again often bound with silver wire, both to embellish and to strengthen.

Most of the corkscrews described above are about three inches long, but tiny examples were also made, often with silver screws. Originally used for extracting the corks of perfume bottles, and often still to be found in ladies' travelling dressing cases, these too are prized today.

The second type of eighteenth-century travelling corkscrew was the 'folding bow', the iron screw pivoting to rest inside a bow-shaped silver

88 Five George III travelling corkscrews, all made in Birmingham in the late eighteenth and early nineteenth centuries. Each screw is protected by a tapering silver sheath. The T-shaped handles were made from many different materials, including: ivory, mother-of-pearl, silver, and enamelled copper. £400-£600.

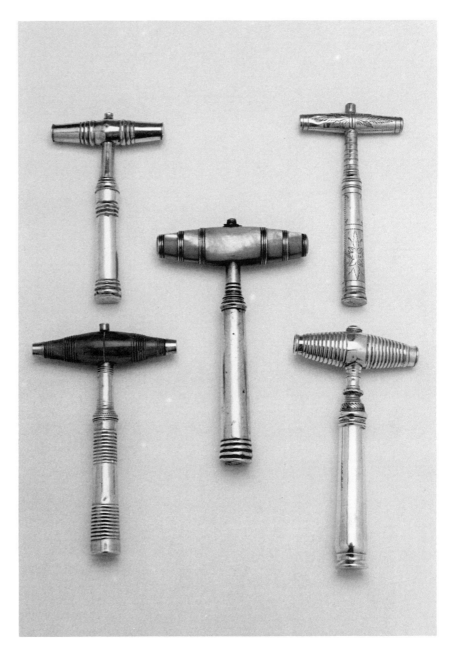

handle when not in use. They were made throughout the eighteenth century and well into the nineteenth with little change to the design. As most were unmarked, they are notoriously difficult to date, their primitive and functional appearance suggesting a much earlier period than their actual date of manufacture.

Some rare eighteenth-century corkscrews incorporate nutmeg graters. These were formerly a standard fitting in canteens used for both peacetime travelling and military campaigns. The earliest shape of these curiosities was the 'mace-shape', with an acorn-shaped grater attached to

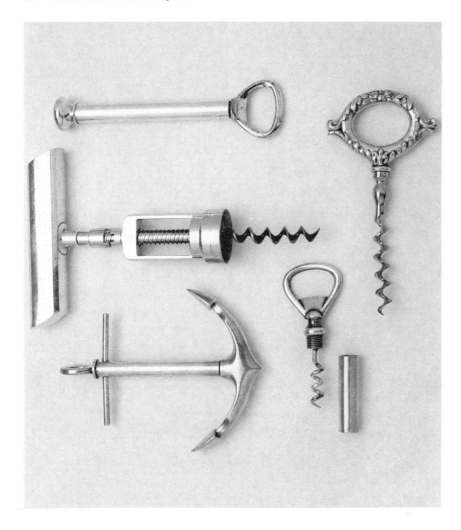

89 Selection of turn-of-the-century American corkscrews, two examples with bottle-opener handles. £100-£150.

the sheath by a screw thread, the grater serving as the handle for the corkscrew. This style earned its name partly because of its resemblance to the traditional sceptre-shaped staff of office carried as a symbol of authority in civic and national ceremonial processions. The second reason for this style undoubtedly relates to a rather dubious pun, mace being an alternative term for nutmeg. These corkscrews are sturdy, the silver components often surviving in excellent condition, although the tip of the iron screw may well be damaged. During the last forty years of the eighteenth century a more graceful, vase-shaped variety of the combination corkscrew and nutmeg grater became fashionable. These often had bright-cut decoration or were engraved with wriggle-work friezes, but being made from much thinner sheet silver, examples in good condition are now scarce.

Although most large eighteenth-century corkscrews were made of brass and iron, a few, very rare exceptions had silver mounts. These are now undoubtedly the aristocrats of this recent area of collecting. Some mechanical corkscrews of the 'Farrow and Jackson' type, with butterfly

90 *Left:* rare, early eighteenth-century combination corkscrew and nutmeg grater formed as a mace; unmarked, £800-£1,000; *right:* travelling corkscrew by Samuel Pemberton, Birmingham, 1790, in poor condition, with a worn ivory handle, split silver mount, and bruised sheath, £150-£200.

91 Rare 'Farrow and Jackson' type corkscrew by James Kidder, London, 1802, engraved with an original crest. While brass examples cost £300-£400 each, this unusual silver piece would retail for at least £4,000.

92 *Left:* silver-handled simple corkscrew by I.R., London, 1789, £600-£800; *right:* pocket corkscrew, the sheath designed to pass through the loop to form a T-shaped handle. Made in London in 1836, the marks are badly struck onto the loop so the maker cannot be identified. £500-£700.

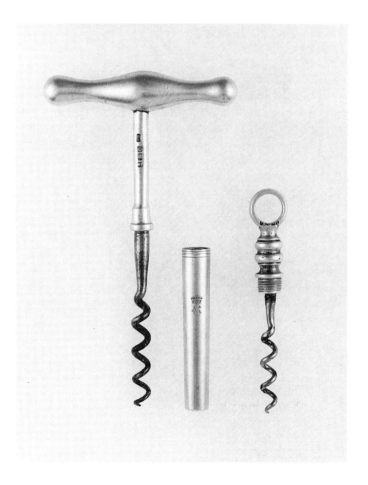

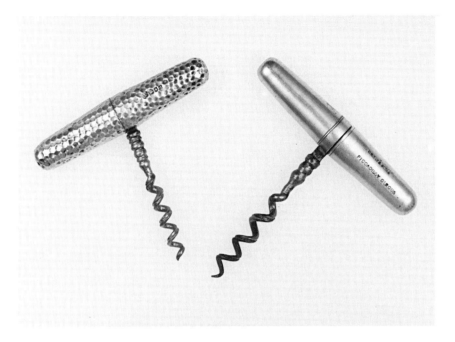

93 Two late nineteenth-century 'picnic' corkscrews, the steel screws folding back inside the torpedo-shaped handles when not in use. *Left:* A.C., London, 1899, £150-£200; *right:* unmarked, although stamped with a retailer's name: Drew and Sons, Piccadilly Circus, £80-£100.

nuts and open cages, were made in silver, their screws and driving mechanisms made from iron. The earliest known example was hall-marked in London in 1796, but the design continued in manufacture well into the reign of Queen Victoria. Survivors made before 1820 are extremely rare, and a George III specimen would be very expensive.

The nineteenth century saw the introduction of a new type of travelling corkscrew, its steel screw concealed inside a torpedo or cigar-shaped case. This unscrewed at the centre to allow the screw to pivot, the two halves of the case reassembling to form a T-shaped handle. Usually known as 'picnic screws', their silver cases were often stamped with elaborate floral designs, or simply turned with reeding.

Many larger nineteenth- and twentieth-century simple corkscrews also had silver-mounted handles, usually decorated with stamped vines, scrolls, and bacchanalian figures. Tiffany and Co. and Black, Starr and Gorham of America produced attractive specimens which are now very popular, especially if marked. Other simple corkscrews were fashioned from silver-mounted hunting trophies such as boars' tusks and antelope horns both here and in America, and I have even seen pieces made from preserved stags' feet. They generally had plain band mounts which were sometimes engraved with monograms and dates.

Finally, corkscrews were made *en suite* with bottle openers in the 1920s and 1930s. The sets were often cased and had geometric engine-turned decoration in keeping with the Art Deco taste. Despite the current vogue for 1930s designs, it should still be possible to find a boxed set quite easily, although the mark of a collected maker such as Georg Jensen, or a popular retailer like Asprey or Cartier might well add a premium to the price.

Wine Funnels

Wine, whether purchased by the barrel or in coarse glass bottles, had to be decanted for table use. To ease this task, silver funnels were developed in the third quarter of the seventeenth century. Survivors from this early period are rare, and most wine funnels available to the collector date from a century later.

Early funnels were plain and sturdy, with straight, tapering spigots and simple conical bowls. One assumes that they were filled with muslin to strain any impurities from the wine. By the mid 1700s funnels were usually made in two sections, the upper bowl pierced with small holes to filter pieces of cork and other impurities from the wine. Many also had a detachable rim pierced with a circle of smaller holes, so that muslin could be attached and used to filter out fine sediment. The spigot acquired a curved tip so that the wine passing through the funnel would gently run down the side of the container, thus avoiding aeration of the valuable liquid, which might lead to deterioration. From the 1770s most funnels had a small plain or shell-shaped clip soldered to the rim of the bowl, the function of which now seems obscure. In *The Book of Wine Antiques* by Robin Butler and Gillian Walkling it is suggested that this enabled the bowl to be used separately, for straining punch or tea, but it could also have been used to hang the funnel after washing, thus ensuring that no traces of water would remain to contaminate the next bottle of wine.

The wine connoisseur or collector of antique silver would be advised to try and find a funnel from the late eighteenth century, as the rarity of earlier examples ensures very high prices. Late eighteenth- and nineteenth-century funnels vary in shape and decoration. Early examples had applied rims with bead or gadroon mounts to give strength. From 1800 the shallow bowls gradually deepened, the addition of chased fluting a common feature used both to decorate and strengthen. By 1825 most funnels had deeply-fluted, compressed bowls echo-

94 Four late eighteenth- and early nineteenth-century wine funnels, the earliest, second from the left, made in Dublin, 1771. Notice the clips, from which the funnels could be hung after washing, and the curved spigots, designed to make the wine run gently down the side of the decanter to avoid aeration. £400-£600.

95 George III funnel and stand by Emes and Barnard, London, 1812. Although they match in date and decoration, they are engraved with different initials. This would imply that they were not actually made to go together, but have been paired up at a later date. £700-£900.

ing the popular 'melon fluting' of the period normally associated with tea and coffee services. Funnels were now larger and often had elaborate shell and scroll rims. Although American funnels followed the same lines of development as their English counterparts, Scottish examples were sometimes of oval section, a much rarer form, enhancing the value by some fifty per cent.

In the late eighteenth and early nineteenth centuries small circular stands with slightly-raised centres were made to accompany wine funnels. Presumably used to prevent the wine from marking a polished table, they are now quite difficult to find. Most are incompletely marked as they were meant to be used with their fully-marked funnels. English funnel stands are particularly rare, and most of the surviving examples were made in Scotland or Ireland.

Bottle Tickets, Rings, and Corks

Wine and spirit labels, known as 'bottle tickets' in the eighteenth century, first appeared in the mid 1730s, possibly replacing earlier parchment labels stuck directly onto the glass bottles. It is now generally agreed that the first silver labels were escutcheon or cartouche-shaped, each formed from a series of symmetrical scrolls and curved to hang smoothly against the bottle. Most were quite plain, although some examples were flat-chased with scrolling vines around the name of the wine. Many early labels bear only a maker's mark, as each weighed less than ten penny-weights. They were thus excluded from hallmarking until 1784, when new regulations were introduced. The most commonly found initials, SD, with a crown above, are those of Sandilands Drinkwater, a London silversmith who entered this mark in 1731. No collection of labels is complete without an example of his production, so the price for a good Drinkwater label is high.

In the 1740s and 1750s new possibilities in both shape and decoration were explored. Gadrooned, oblong labels with both straight and curved edges made their appearance as did cast labels moulded and chased with rococo putti and satyrs' masks amidst vines, the name of the wine engraved on a scroll in the middle of the label. Labels from this period are rare, possibly because of the large numbers of attractive enamel specimens made by the Battersea factory between 1753 and 1756. Bright and colourful, these flooded the market in the mid eighteenth century, their popularity almost rendering the silver label obsolete.

After the bankruptcy of the Battersea factory in 1756, the silver label soared back into fashion. During the last forty years of the eighteenth century, many thousands of delightful examples were produced by both specialist and general silversmiths. Even the most elevated and skilful makers such as Paul Storr did not scorn the humble bottle ticket, although examples by the more celebrated craftsmen will be beyond the reach of most collectors, often costing many hundreds of pounds. Nevertheless, one can find numerous specimens of a more simple nature produced from thin sheet metal. Many were enlivened with bright-cut engraving or had applied beaded edges, while others had delightful feather designs engraved on their rims. The last quarter of the eighteenth century also saw the introduction of miniature labels for condiment bottles, now collected in their own right. Condiment labels followed the shape and decoration of their larger counterparts, but are usually no bigger than three quarters of an inch in diameter.

96 Selection of labels, all late eighteenth- or early nineteenth-century, showing just a few of the great variety of styles available to the collector. £50-£80 each.

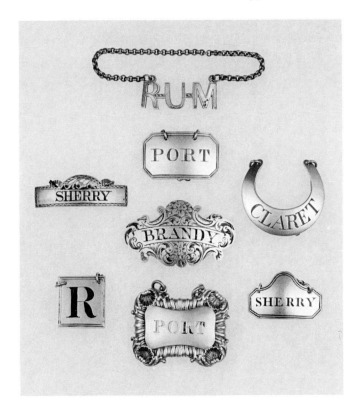

97 Two Victorian enamelled initial labels by Reily and Storer, London, 1850, and two sherry labels, the quatrefoil example by Thomas Jenkins, London, 1858. The rare, bat-shaped label is unmarked, but it has been suggested that this and similar pieces were probably made in India, for the European market. £50-£150.

Most labels of this period were engraved with the name of the wine or spirit, but rarer examples had pierced lettering, subsequently damaged and then repaired with small blobs of solder. Unusual pieces also have a cut-out crest surmount, or incorporate a cartouche into their design, often engraved with the crest or initials of the original owner. Such labels are much collected. Although many labels had hand-raised decoration, cheaper die-stamped versions were available from 1793, when Matthew Linwood of Birmingham introduced a process which enabled many pieces to be struck cheaply and quickly from thin sheet metal. He and other silversmiths produced some fine, intricate designs with sharp, detailed patterns.

At the beginning of the nineteenth century, the simple label cut from sheet silver lost much of its popularity, and was largely replaced by a heavier design cast in metal, often decorated in high relief with vines,

98 Set of unusual labels with suspension loops of wire, instead of the more standard chains. Made by Phipps and Robinson, London, 1796, and in excellent condition, this set would now retail for £1,500-£2,000.

99 *Top:* four Victorian initial labels by Rawlins and Sumner, London, 1859 and 1860, £350-£450; *bottom:* three George III cast shell labels by Benjamin and James Smith, London, 1811, £1,000-£1,200.

foliage, human and animal masks, and bacchanalian putti. Many were further enhanced with gilding. These cast labels proved to be too expensive for many buyers, so cheaper, die-stamped versions continued to be made in large quantities.

Another popular shape was the vine leaf, generally pierced with the name of the wine and usually die-stamped, although cast examples can be found. These were introduced by Charles Rawlins of London in 1824, and remained popular well into the reign of Queen Victoria. Single vine leaves are quite common, but examples formed from two or more leaves are much rarer, and consequently more expensive.

Initial labels were introduced in the 1830s and most were heavily cast and chased with elaborate scrolling foliage and flowers, although plain examples may also be found. These seem to be currently less popular than other labels. The scallop shell shape was also adapted by the Victorian silversmiths, who produced heavy cast labels with pierced lettering, now in great demand. The mid nineteenth century saw the introduction of novelty labels made in India from silver-mounted boars' tusks and tigers' claws and teeth, applied with the name of a wine or spirit. These grisly relics of our ancestors' hunting exploits are perhaps a little macabre for today's taste. Curious labels in the form of bats were also introduced at this time. Invariably unmarked but probably Indian in origin, they are very popular today.

Wine labels ceased to be made in any quantity after 1860, when the Licensing Act made it legal for shops to sell single bottles of alcoholic beverages, with the added obligation that each bottle had to carry a pasted paper label denoting its contents. Spirits were still decanted however, so labels were still manufactured, many of them copying earlier gadrooned oblong designs.

Although most labels had fine silver chains, some examples were made with sprung wires, the label suspended from a single, central loop instead of having holes drilled through the two upper corners. A further variation of the wine label is the bottle collar, a circular ring of silver designed to drop neatly over the neck of the bottle, coming to rest on its shoulders. These were often quite plain, although some had simple reeded or feather-engraved borders, and were normally pierced with the name of the wine. Dating from the 1770s, they are now rather scarce.

Some bottles were marked with silver-mounted corks, usually with a small disc or ring engraved with the name of the wine. Heavier cast examples decorated with scallop shells and scrolls can also be found. Most named bottle corks date from the 1780s to around 1830, although later specimens decorated with die-stamped cherubs, animals' heads, and vines were still popular in the Edwardian period. Late, mass-produced corks seem to attract little demand. Georgian corks are much more saleable.

Some buyers collect the names rather than the labels, delighting in finding strange, obsolete labels for beverages such as Brown Bang, Captain's White, and Old Tom, or searching out quaint spelling mistakes like Clairret, Clarret, and Clart. *The Book of Wine Antiques* gives almost five hundred different names of wines to be found on antique labels, their comprehensive list not including spirit names such as Cream of the Valley, Hollands, and Nig (all euphemisms for gin) or condiment names such as Catsup, Lemon, and Anchovy. Obviously, one will never find genuine, antique labels engraved with more modern drinks such as Rye or Bourbon, although some are re-engraved, to entrap the unwary buyer.

100 George III cruet made in 1796, the bottles with tiny labels made by Phipps and Robinson of London. Individual condiment labels can still be found for £30–£50.

Spirit Flasks, and Tot Cups and Bottles

Portable glass flasks were introduced in the late eighteenth century, and the silversmiths soon recognized the need to protect this fragile material with metal mounts. Examples made before the 1830s are rare and most of the flasks available to the modern collector are of Victorian and Edwardian manufacture. They are either made entirely of silver or with cut-glass bodies and silver screw tops, often with bayonet fittings and interior corks, to ensure a leak-proof closure. Both types have gilt-lined detachable cups, to facilitate more elegant drinking.

Most eighteenth- and early nineteenth-century flasks were of oval or oblong section. The curved flask designed to fit snugly into the pocket became popular towards the end of the nineteenth century. Good, heavy flasks are popular today, particularly if decorated with spot hammering or engine-turning, as these disguise any scratches or minor damage. A few flasks were enhanced with enamelling, but this is now often badly chipped or scratched. One unusual piece to look out for is the combination flask and cheroot case, a hinged lid opening to reveal a concealed compartment. Mostly made at the turn of the century, these are now uncommon.

Solid silver flasks with small dents can be repaired if they are filled with water and then placed in a deep-freezer. As the water turns to ice it expands, forcing out the malleable metal to its correct shape. One must be careful with this however, as too much water can split the silver along the join lines, breaking the solder and forcing apart the two halves of the flask.

Some amusing flasks engraved with wry comments were made in America during the prohibition period. An example sold by Christie's of South Kensington in 1985 was decorated with an elaborate facsimile doctor's prescription dated 3 January 1927, enabling 'Major Frank M. Ballard of 9, Avery Ct, Santa Barbara' to purchase alcohol for medical purposes. A great novelty, this sold for £480.

Silver tot or liqueur cups were normally made in sets of six or more, many deriving their shapes from eighteenth-century porringers and loving-cups. Other examples had pierced and stamped holders fitted with tiny glasses. This latter type were often made on the continent and had import hallmarks. Both kinds of tot cups are illustrated in the 1929 Harrods catalogue, the former priced at £5 17s. 6d., the latter at £3 3s. 0d. for sets of six, each 'in velvet-lined case'. Although individual specimens

101 Two American nineteenth-century flasks: *left* to *right:* Tiffany and Co., New York, *c.* 1898, £200–£300; Tiffany and Co., New York, *c.* 1885, £250–£350.

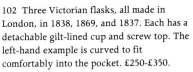

102 Three Victorian flasks, all made in London, in 1838, 1869, and 1837. Each has a detachable gilt-lined cup and screw top. The left-hand example is curved to fit comfortably into the pocket. £250-£350.

103 Whisky tot bottles were made in several shapes, the conical being the most common. Each should have a tiny label suspended from a fine chain, but, unfortunately, these are all too often lost. £70-£100.

are inexpensive, cased sets are far more saleable. Do not be deterred by examples with broken or missing glass. Although this should certainly provide an excellent excuse to haggle and reduce the price, replacement glasses can be obtained quite cheaply in clear, ruby, and 'Bristol blue', usually available in stock sizes from manufacturers of salt cellar liners.

Silver-mounted glass whisky tot bottles made from the turn of the century to the 1940s can still be found quite easily. Each originally had a small, kidney-shaped label hung around its neck, but many of these are now lost. Several different shapes were manufactured, the most common being the conical and the dimple, both illustrated here.

5 Bedroom and Bathroom Silver

Mirrors, Brushes, and other Silver-Mounted Objects

Silver dressing-table pieces first appeared in the late 1600s, although small pots and jars survive from even earlier periods. Complete sets with brushes, mirrors, trays, candlesticks, and boxes are now extremely rare and costly. A twelve-piece silver-gilt service made in 1683 and decorated with splendid chased foliage and classical scenes, was sold in 1982 by Christies in New York for £245,882 and Christies of London obtained a bid of £2,000 for a pair of small circular boxes auctioned in 1977. Fortunately there are still numerous examples of bedroom and bathroom silver available in a lower price range.

Eighteenth-century artifacts are relatively uncommon, but the nineteenth century saw the introduction of a vast range of dressing-table items, many made of silver or with silver mounts. Manufacturers took advantage of mass-production techniques to create attractive but flimsy bedroom ornaments, much collected today. Stocks are being constantly replenished as the contents of dressing cases are split up, because most small dealers find that a better profit can be made by selling each item separately.

In the late nineteenth century the wooden dressing case was largely replaced by leather or crocodile suitcases containing a variety of silver and silver-mounted fittings. The contents were often smothered with a confused mass of flowers, birds, masks, and scrolling foliage, the exuberance of decoration giving a misleading impression of quality and weight. In fact, most were lined with solidified pitch. Vast numbers of dressing-table pieces in this style were made, but today it is rare to find examples in good condition.

At the turn of the century, Art Nouveau sets became popular, often decorated with delightful female masks with flowing hair, or with stylised flowers and leaves. Both American and British examples can still be found quite easily. One of the most popular motives was a charming design of five cherubs' heads peering out through a bank of woolly clouds. This was based on the paintings of Angelica Kauffmann, an eighteenth-century Swiss artist who specialized in rather sugary neo-classical pieces often used to decorate house interiors. Her work obviously appealed to the sentimental Victorians, judging from the large amount of silver decorated in this manner which survives today.

The early twentieth century favoured much plainer sets, their mounts often engine-turned or covered with bright guilloche enamelling. Others were backed with a combination of silver and tortoiseshell, often inlaid with delicate ribbon and floral swags and wreaths. These later pieces are often in better condition today, as their silver mounts were usually of a slightly thicker gauge. Nevertheless, they seem relatively unpopular, and perfect specimens are available for small sums of money.

Although many small dealers split up the contents of dressing cases for resale to the public, one can still buy a complete set at auction. Leather cases are usually in little demand, as they are too heavy for modern air travel. Crocodile-skin cases are far more saleable, even if lacking their original fittings. While most cases are of typical suitcase form, one can also find numerous examples of the Gladstone bag. This variation, named after the celebrated British Prime Minister, closely resembles a carpet bag or old-fashioned doctor's bag. It has two hinged lids which lock at the centre, each normally fitted with compartments to hold brushes and toilet jars, and a large space beneath for clothing. These bags were popular for over-night trips, enabling everything necessary for a short visit to be packed into a compact and readily portable container. Today they seem to be enjoying a revival.

More comprehensive dressing-table sets often contained buttonhooks, shoe horns, and glove-stretchers. These are all now collected, and there is even a specialist club for the button-hook enthusiast. Both button-hooks and shoe horns were certainly made in the early seventeenth century. Their early history is obscure however, and the collector

104 Rare Victorian glove powderer by George Fox, London, 1887, £250-£300.

105 Selection of turn-of-the-century button hooks, mainly with silver handles. The larger examples were used for shoes and boots, while the smaller hooks were used for gloves and collars. Shoe horns and manicure implements have similar handles stamped out in thin metal filled with pitch. £15-£40.

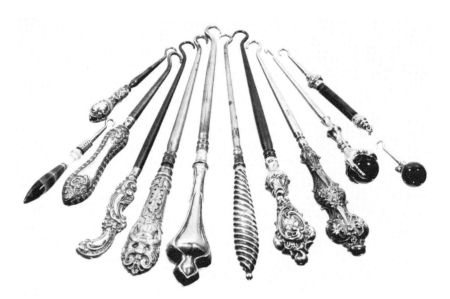

106 Three pieces from an American late nineteenth-century bedroom set by Mauser, c. 1900, each stamped with sentimental cherubs and rococo swags. This type of decoration was typical of the period, both in Britain and The United States. £50-£150.

will find that most of the silver-handled examples currently available date from the late nineteenth and early twentieth centuries. Fashions of this period demanded high buttoned boots for both men and women, women also wearing elbow-length gloves and high-necked dresses, all fastened with rows of tiny buttons. Victorian etiquette demanded that gloves should be worn on all occasions. This was explained in a letter published in 1862 in *The Queen*, an influential magazine read by many middle-class women. The letter stated: 'In every costume but the most extreme negligé a lady cannot be said to be dressed except she is nicely and completely gloved; and this applies equally to morning, afternoon, dinner and evening dress'. Only working women would have rough, chapped, or sun-burnt hands, and ladies were expected to have tiny, pure white hands free from callouses and blemishes.

Many wealthy women also insisted on forcing their hands into gloves which were too small, thus giving themselves a deceptively dainty appearance. Silver-handled ebony and ivory glove-stretchers were developed for this purpose, their scissor-action stretching the supple kid-skin fingers of the gloves so that they could be put on with greater ease. The insides of the fingers were also dusted with talcum powder sprinkled from small containers. These were similar to salt or pepper pots, although they usually had elongated, slender necks, to enable the tips of the fingers to be dusted. Thus lubricated, the tight gloves could be squeezed onto chubby hands, with the added advantage that the powder would absorb the moisture from clammy palms.

The first World War heralded the beginning of the end for both button-hooks and glove-stretchers. As more and more men were called up for military service, their original jobs were filled by women. Even the wealthy went out to work, driving ambulances, spending many hours cutting sandwiches or washing up in canteens staffed largely by volunteers. The wearing of gloves during the day became impractical, although evening wear still demanded that long gloves should be worn, many, no doubt, now concealing chaffed skin and broken finger-nails.

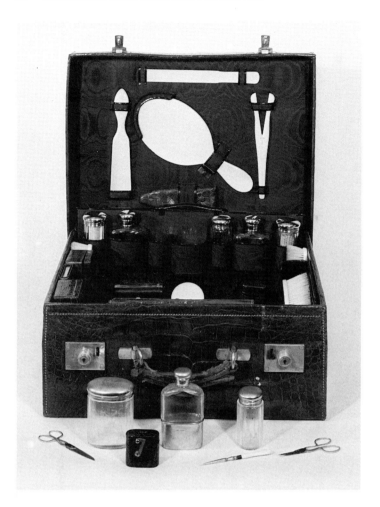

107 Expensive cases contained a wide range of fittings, as can be seen here. Most are now too heavy for modern air travel, and are subsequently broken up, their contents sold off individually by the trade. This set, by Mappin and Webb, Sheffield, 1935, has an attractive crocodile case worth £400-£600, while the fittings might sell for several hundreds of pounds.

108 Small dressing table sets were popular birthday and engagement gifts. One can still find a great many in good condition, and they therefore tend to be very inexpensive. The set illustrated is better than most, as it is inset with finely-painted Royal Worcester porcelain plaques. S.and M., Birmingham, 1928, £600-£800

When the war was over, fashions changed dramatically. The languid and delicate debutante was largely replaced by the flapper, a boyish hoyden determined to keep a firm grip on her new independence. The final blow was struck with the introduction into 'respectable society'of smoking for women. Gloves were now eschewed even for evening wear, as they interfered with this new craze. Although some dressing cases made in the 1940s still contained shoe horns, button-hooks, and glove-stretchers, these are now unusual. Most pieces date from the 1890-1930 period.

Novelty examples with embossed figural terminals were also popular, and attract much interest today. Owls, herons, swans, teddy bears, Punch and Judy, jesters, and lions can still be found, many with tiny paste eyes. While most specimens were fully hallmarked, many bearing the stamps of the Birmingham and Chester assay offices, unmarked examples are not uncommon. Of these, a number were manufactured in Ireland and Scotland, their decoration often incorporating tiny Connemara marble harps and shamrocks or agate thistles. Presumably originally sold as tourists' souvenirs, these attractive pieces are in less demand than their hallmarked counterparts.

Toilet Jars and Bottles

Silver-topped glass toilet jars and bottles seem to have made their first appearance in the early nineteenth century. Most brass-bound wooden dressing cases contained several examples, their sturdy screw tops often engine-turned or bright-cut with arabesques. Many circular specimens are no more than one and a half inches in diameter, and were presumably designed to hold salves and ointments. Larger, upright bottles for liquids such as cologne were also quite standard, often with unmarked silver tops concealing tiny ground and faceted glass stoppers. The latter were supposed to ensure an air-tight fit, this preventing possible leakage or

109 Selection of turn-of-the-century cologne bottles, the most elaborate example on the right made by William Comyns, London, 1892. £150-£200 each, although a pair might well cost £600-£800.

110 Part of a set made by Mappin and Webb, London, 1932, decorated with bright pink enamelling, £20-£80 per bottle.

111 Three American toilet jars overlaid with delicate scrollwork. Two are unmarked, but the Art Nouveau example on the right was made by Black, Starr and Frost. All were manufactured *c.* 1900, £100–£250.

evaporation of the expensive and volatile contents. Georgian jars and bottles are still common, and perfect specimens with clear hallmarks can be found quite easily. Many are remarkably plain, and it has been suggested that these pieces were primarily for masculine use. Certainly, they can often be found in dressing cases, along with boot-pulls, spirit flasks, and razors.

By the mid nineteenth century few 'respectable' gentlewomen would openly use cosmetics to improve their complexions. 'Painted faces' had become synonomous with harlots and actresses. Nevertheless, despite their affectations of 'natural beauty', many women used artificial aids in private. Magazines contained many 'tried and tested' recipes for home-made creams and lotions, along with advertisements for commercially-produced face powders, rouges, and skin tonics. Although these cosmetics became increasingly popular, the guilt attached to their use remained for many years. Few ladies dared to flaunt their 'shamelessness' by displaying pots and jars on their dressing-tables, thus advertising their dependence upon such artifices.

Less hypocrisy was attached to perfume, although heavy, musky scents were frowned upon, as being redolent of the harem houri. In his 1867 *Book of Perfume* Eugene Rimmel wrote: 'Above all, avoid strong, coarse perfumes and remember that if a woman's temper may be told from her handwriting, her good taste and breeding may as easily be ascertained by the perfume she wears'. Light, flowery scents such as lavender water and eau-de-cologne were permissable in Britain, while 'respectable' nineteenth-century American women used Florida water, a perfume with a similar delicate fragrance. Many of these scents were home-made, following family recipes passed down from generation to generation. These would require decanting into pretty bottles, as would professionally made colognes, often sold in unattractive containers resembling chemists' bottles. Consequently, large dressing-table bottles made from cut-glass and silver were produced in great quantities during the last half of the nineteenth century, their manufacture persisting until about 1930 although twentieth-century examples are less common. Many measured six to eight inches in height. Frequently sold in pairs, they are much collected today.

More elaborate spherical cologne bottles had pierced and stamped mounts, which extended to cover the upper half of the body with a delicate filigree pattern. Although most were decorated with typically Victorian flowers and leaves, others had lids stamped with classical or biblical subjects surrounded by rococo shells and scrolls, based on designs for mid eighteenth-century watch cases.

While the British seemed to prefer the rather splendidly heavy combination of cut-glass and silver, the Americans favoured more delicate designs, often manufactured in coloured glass. Spherical bottles were overlaid with thin sterling silver mounts, actually pressed into the glass and often finely engraved. Art Nouveau styles were especially popular at the turn of the century, and many examples were entirely covered with charming stylized flowers such as poppies, lilies, and thistles. Sadly, most specimens are unmarked or simply impressed 'sterling', this intimating manufacture in America while failing to identify both date and maker.

By the 1880s the heavy cut-glass cologne bottle began to be replaced by cheaper alternatives, often made of moulded glass or cut with more simple fluted or ribbed designs. Moulded glass examples are often difficult to identify as some makers would mould and then cut, adding depth and sharpness to mass-produced decoration to give an impression of greater quality. Moulded bottles should be cheaper than their cut-glass counterparts. In fact, they seem to attract almost as much interest.

During the first decades of the twentieth century cosmetics became more socially acceptable, perhaps because several influential members of the aristocracy chose to marry actresses who introduced new ideas into a rather stuffy society. Toilet jars and bottles were now produced in ever increasing numbers to satisfy the demand. Some lavish dressing cases contained over a dozen different pots with thin silver mounts and lids, other pots merely had simple collars cemented to their necks. These are frequently in poor condition now, their mounts bruised or loose. Many shapes and sizes of toilet jars were made, ranging from tiny rouge pots to large powder bowls, sometimes still containing a swan's down powder puff and with a mirror glued to the inside of the lid. Jars with circular apertures in their lids are also quite common. These are 'hair tidies', originally used to contain hair removed from one's brush. This would be carefully saved for eventual use in the manufacture of false hair-pieces, as so many elaborate Victorian and Edwardian hair styles called for additional curls, plaits, and chignons.

Trinket Trays and Boxes

Trinket and jewellery trays and boxes were produced for seventeenth- and eighteenth-century toilet services, although early pieces are now rare and very costly. Victorian, Edwardian, and later examples are far more common. They are popular and quite expensive, selling for considerably more than the brushes and mirrors which once accompanied them.

Dressing-table trays were made in two main sizes, with ten to twelve inch examples for displaying brushes, and three to four inch 'pin-trays' for small trinkets and jewellery. They were usually made from either thin stamped silver, or from swag-inlaid tortoiseshell trays with silver rim mounts. Many specimens bear hallmarks from Birmingham or Chester, although the prolific maker William Comyns produced numerous examples, generally assayed in London.

Trinket boxes for dressing-table use were produced in large numbers at the turn of the century. Many were lined with coloured plush or velvet, the more elaborate had interior divisions and trays for rings and other pieces of jewellery. Tiny boxes designed to hold a single ring are now popular, especially if heart-shaped. Larger boxes were often made of silver-mounted wood, their pierced and stamped mounts closely resembling those found on contemporary stationary boxes or desk blotters (see chapter 6).

The Edwardian era saw the introduction of small circular or oblong boxes standing on cabriole legs, often with tortoiseshell lids inlaid with swags and paterae. The contrast between the rich browns of the tortoiseshell and the silver mounts is most attractive, so perfect examples sell very well. Some larger circular and oval trinket boxes have padded pin-cushion lids originally covered in richly-coloured velvet matching the moire silk interior fittings. These boxes often have simple slat-pierced mounts made from thinly-rolled silver, closely resembling wine coasters in both size and decoration. Indeed, Georgian coasters were often converted into jewellery boxes at the turn of the century. Edwardian boxes

112 Inexpensive, small trinket box by H.M., Birmingham, 1903. Three inches long. £100-£120.

113 Three jewellery boxes: *left* to *right*: unmarked electro-plate, *c.* 1870, £200-£250; silver and tortoiseshell, William Comyns, London, 1894, £400-£500; silver, C.S.and F.S., Chester, 1908, £400-£500.

114 Two pin cushion trinket boxes: *left to right:* L.and S., Birmingham, 1913, £70-£100; William Comyns, London, 1892, £100-£120. Worn tops can be replaced easily and effectively, using richly-coloured velvet.

115 An excellent silver and tortoiseshell trinket box inlaid and applied with swags. William Comyns, London, 1902, £700-£1,000.

116 Three late nineteenth-century trinket trays with stamped decoration, the largest by J.D. and W.D., Chester, 1898. The two narrower examples are both American, *c.* 1900. *Left:* Gorham; *right:* Tiffany and Co., £100-£400.

of this type seem to be less saleable than those with elaborately-pierced and stamped mounts, and, as coasters have become so desirable today, many boxes have been reconverted.

Novelty jewellery boxes in the shape of Georgian bow-fronted sideboards became popular in the early twentieth century. Their hinged covers open to reveal divisions for rings and other small pieces of jewellery. Many had false drawer fronts and cupboard doors, although occasionally one may come across an example fitted with tiny velvet-lined drawers which actually open, each designed to hold one ring.

Although valuable jewellery was often kept locked away, many ladies had ring-trees on their dressing tables. These had several branches designed to hold half a dozen rings. Some were mounted onto shallow bowls, presumably to hold other small pieces of jewellery. Many ring-trees were actually modelled as miniature trees, the silver stamped to

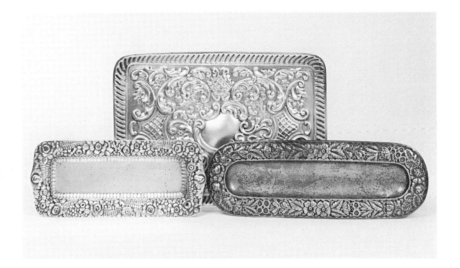

resemble bark, others were formed as hands with outstretched fingers, or as branches of coral.

During the late nineteenth and early twentieth centuries, fashion dictated the wearing of enormous hats heavily bedecked with feathers, stuffed birds, silk flowers, and artificial fruit. They were secured by means of formidable steel hat-pins, often fitted with a safety knob to prevent their sharp tips from inflicting dangerous wounds. Many hat-pins had silver decorative terminals pierced with scroll-work and enlivened with enamelling. Others had novelty terminals formed as tennis racquets or golf clubs, presumably designed for those emancipated young women who took up sports at the turn of the century. Today hat-pins are little collected, perhaps because they are unwearable in their original form, although some specimens have been cut down, the steel pins shortened and resharpened to form tie-pins. These can be spotted quite easily, as most genuine tie-pins were made with gold or silver wire.

Hat-pin stands have stuffed pin cushion bases, sometimes filled with emery to maintain the sharpness of the steel pins, although sawdust was also used. They generally have a central column similar in design to a ring-tree, although instead of branches the column is decked with wirework loops which support the weight of the hat-pins. Both elaborate pins and stands ceased to be made in large numbers during the first World War, when enormous hats became impractical and unfashionable.

117 *Left:* ring trees sell well today, although most are flimsy in construction. This specimen, made by W.A., Birmingham, 1912, has an extra feature: a hook from which a small watch can be suspended. £70-£100.

118 *Right:* golfing ring tree and hatpin stand, made by C.C., Birmingham, 1909, and a set of tennis racquet manicure implements, made by C.and Co., Chester, 1930. £200-£250 each.

Miscellaneous Bedroom and Bathroom Silver

119 Curious Victorian scent spray formed as a watering can. This two and a half inch novelty, by Samuel Watton Smith, London, 1882, sold for £280 at auction. £400-£500.

120 Collection of miniature hand mirrors, mainly early twentieth-century. The example on the left, made by T. D., London, 1840, has a folding handle. Designed to be easily portable, three have tiny loops so that they can hang from a chatelaine. £20-£80.

One might imagine that a bedroom would be well and truly cluttered with silver, considering the amount and variety of items already described in this chapter. Dressing-tables were smothered with decorative, useful pieces, arranged and displayed rather like prizes on a fairground stall. Unbelievably, there are even more silver bedroom knick-knacks, some dealt with in other chapters. Photograph frames (pp. 120-1), clocks (pp. 123-4), and vases (pp. 70-1) were all used in the bedrooms and dressing rooms of the wealthy, and dressing tables were often supplied with dwarf candlesticks (p. 120).

Manicure sets with silver mounts were produced in large numbers at the turn of the century, some sold in separate fitted boxes and others supplied as parts of larger dressing table sets. They usually contained nail files, scissors, polishers or buffers, and tiny silver-topped cut-glass

jars. The 1929 Harrods catalogue illustrated three styles ranging from £1. 10s. 0d. to £4. 10s. 0d. in price, the more expensive decorated with a choice of pink, blue, or mauve enamelling. Separate nail polishers with cut-glass bowls were also available. Plain examples cost 14s. 6d. but engine-turned pieces retailed for 17s. 6d.

In the 1860s womens' hair styles became far more elaborate. Waves and curls were now *de rigueur*, and ladies' maids were expected to keep up with new fashions, often introduced from the continent. Hair was usually curled using silver-handled steel tongs. Folding curling tongs were made for travelling purposes, and many luxury dressing cases contained silver-mounted spirit burners to heat the blades. I have even seen these in gentlemens' cases, and can only assume that they were used to curl the splendid moustaches and beards so fashionable in the second half of the nineteenth century.

121 Manicure set by Mappin and Webb, London, 1925, including two small pots for cream and a nail buffer covered in soft suede. £70-£100.

122 More unusual manicure set on a stand with swivelling mirror, made by H.and H., Birmingham, 1927, £180-£220.

123 Bright-cut toothpowder box, toothbrush, and tongue scraper by Joseph Taylor, Birmingham, 1797, with original red leather case. Complete sets like this are now rare. £800-£1,000. *Photograph by courtesy of the Birmingham Assay Office.*

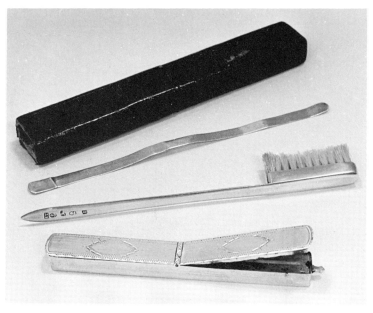

The collector may be puzzled by brushes with long, silver-mounted handles. Their bristles are too soft for hair or clothes, and they are sometimes erroneously described as crumb brushes (see page 75). In fact, these 'bonnet whisks' were originally used to dust and titivate the elaborate feather trimmings and silk ruches and flowers on late Victorian and Edwardian hats. Relatively unpopular today, they can still be found quite easily.

Having discussed silver and silver-mounted items made for bedroom use, one must now consider several pieces created for the bathroom. Late seventeenth- and early eighteenth-century soap boxes were usually spherical, with pierced lids to allow the ball of soap to dry and harden after use. Normally made from heavy gauge silver and resembling an orange in size, these pieces are now avidly collected. Once commonly sold in pairs, with a pierced box for soap and a solid box for wash sponge, good examples with contemporary armorials are now very scarce. Nineteenth-century soap boxes are still available in large numbers however. Most are oval in shape, ideal for modern bars of soap, and again their lids are often pierced. Decoration varied enormously in the Victorian and Edwardian eras. Ladies' boxes were often stamped with full-blown flowers and leaves, while those designed for gentlemen were more plain, the decoration restricted to simple engine-turning or spot-hammering.

Cylindrical holders for shaving soap date from the late eighteenth century, although once again the collector is more likely to find Victorian examples. They were originally made en suite with badger's hair shaving brushes, enclosed in a case when not in use. The hair is cemented into a circular mount and screwed into the case which then forms the handle. One might imagine that such pieces would be very

124 Victorian spot-hammered oval soap box, ideal for a modern tablet of soap and therefore quite expensive. Samuel Watton Smith, Birmingham, 1899, £150-£200.

125 *Left* to *right:* eighteenth-century soap box by John Chapman, London, 1733; soap box and sponge box by John Chantier, London, 1722. These simple but sturdy pieces are now very popular, and one could expect to pay £2,500-£3,000 for a pair in good condition.

unfashionable today, their utility replaced by more modern shaving techniques. However, both antique brushes and soap holders are collected.

Silver shaving mugs were made in both Britain and America, their shape identical to that of the more familiar contemporary pottery cup. Examples were mentioned in late nineteenth-century Tiffany catalogues, some fitted with an 'attachment in which to burn alcohol to heat the water'. On a more humble scale, the 1895 mail-order catalogue of Montgomery Ward and Co. of New York illustrates two gilt-lined silver-plated shaving mugs with matching brushes, decorated with 'elegant satin engraving'. The simplest set cost $3 while the *de luxe* version, the mug with 'removable compartment' for easier cleaning, was priced at $5.50. Antique silver shaving mugs are now difficult to find, and are therefore very expensive.

Toothbrushes were first developed in the mid to late seventeenth century, although early examples bear little relation to modern brushes. Hogs' bristles were tied in small bunches and inserted into primitive hollow handles made from bone or ivory, the resulting brush used to scrub the teeth with a coarse paste. Recipes for tooth-paste included ground cuttle-fish bone, coral, and brick dust, the abrasive mixture sweetened with sugar and perfumed with rose water. It is hardly surprising that most people preferred to clean their teeth by chewing wooden sticks or twigs, sweetening their breath with peppermint or violet-scented cachoux. The late eighteenth century saw the introduction of a new type of toothbrush similar in design to those we still use today. These had long flat handles attached to an oblong frame into which a pad of bristles could be inserted, and one could buy spare pads to replace those which became worn.

The Birmingham 'toy-makers' manufactured many toothbrushes in the 1790s, often sold with bright-cut boxes for toothpowder, long, flexible tongue scrapers, and silver or ivory toothpicks. Sets usually came complete with a leather or shagreen case, although rare toothbrush boxes were also made in silver. These had one end pierced to allow the brush to dry out after use. Smaller boxes were also made to cover the head of the brush. Today it is very difficult to find a complete set, although individual brushes, powder boxes, and tongue-scrapers are more commonly available.

126 Unusual Edwardian silver-mounted razor strop with hanging loop, made by James Dixon and Sons, Sheffield, 1903, £150-£200.

6 Desk Equipment and Accessories

Inkstands and Inkwells

The use of silver in the manufacture of library and study equipment has a very long history. Early desk silver has been collected for many years by antique lovers, and prices have recently soared, due to a desire for impressive offices with valuable and imposing fittings. Fortunately, the nineteenth century saw the introduction of many new desk accessories, both in Britain and America. Few libraries escaped the excessive urge to collect and display, and desks were smothered with 'useful' pieces. Indeed, Queen Victoria's writing-table at Windsor was said to 'resemble a stall at a fancy bazaar'.

The most basic piece of desk equipment was the inkstand. The earliest were formed as oblong trays, normally raised on four feet. Closely resembling cruets, they were fitted with inkwells, wafer boxes, bells, and pounce pots containing powdered gum arabic. This was sprinkled and rubbed onto paper which had been scratched with a knife to erase an error, and served to smooth the surface of the paper preventing blotching. Sanders were introduced in the 1790s. These contained fine sand which was scattered over the page to dry fresh ink.

A near contemporary of the inkstand was the writing box, a casket-shaped container with one or two hinged lids, concealing separate compartments for ink, pounce, and wafers. Many also had a small drawer for quills and pens. Introduced in the Restoration period, they have been much copied in both silver and plate. The originals are now worth many thousands of pounds and even reproductions have become expensive.

The oblong tray inkstand continued to be made for centuries, its basic shape hardly changing, although often enriched with varying forms of decoration. Examples made in the third quarter of the eighteenth century were often galleried, with applied back and side plates pierced and bright-cut. Most had silver-mounted cut-glass bottles and were made from thin sheet silver, which sacrificed quality but, nevertheless gave an impression of magnificence and solidity.

Early nineteenth-century oblong inkstands were often manufactured on a monumental scale in silver-gilt, with fine cast and chased decoration. Designs were inspired by Greek and Egyptian architecture,

127 Two Edwardian novelty inkwells: *left:* massive cut-glass example, the hinged lid inset with a metal 'Goliath' pocket watch, J.C. Vickery, London, 1906, £200-£300; *right:* 'car-lamp' example, the front hinged to hold a watch. Notice that the base has a tiny drawer for stamps. Maker's mark rubbed, Birmingham, 1910, £400-£600.

the end results sometimes ponderous and heavy in spite of the tremendous skills of the silversmiths of this period. Victorian tray inkstands were far lighter in appearance, with stamped scroll and floral borders and feet replacing the cast decoration of the Regency period. Hand workmanship suffered from the introduction of new rolling and pressing machinery, but nevertheless some attractive pieces were made. The metal-workers adapted their designs to mass-production, creating a cheaper inkstand to catch the eye of the growing middle-classes, who could simply not afford to buy expensive, hand-made pieces.

In the 1830s and the 1840s there was a break with the traditional tray inkstand. Frivolous designs were introduced on a large scale, often modelled on natural forms such as animals or flowers. Examples were made for The Great Exhibition of 1851 by silversmiths like the Hennell brothers, and 'the natural imitative style' became much admired, capturing the fancy of the public with its amusing, nonsensical designs. The Edwardians found little to admire in these whimsical pieces however. Their taste was more serious and formal, and their silversmiths revived eighteenth- and early nineteenth-century designs, producing both perfect copies and adaptations, often of excellent quality.

The inkstands described above are all expensive. There are, however, many cheaper and more humble versions available for much smaller sums, produced during the late nineteenth- and early twentieth-centuries to cater to the enormous demand of the middle-classes. The most popular type of inkwell was undoubtedly the 'capstan', produced in large quantities varying in size from two inches to almost one foot. Many thousands must have been made from the turn of the century until well into the 1940s, the majority of them round but with rarer oval, square, hexagonal, and octagonal examples also available to the collector. Small, complete capstan inkwells can still be found quite cheaply,

128 This capstan inkwell is better than most, as the lid is enamelled with a terrier on a cream background. Made in Birmingham, 1912, it has a rubbed maker's mark. £200-£300.

129 Inexpensive four-piece desk set with capstan inkwell, by M.and J., Birmingham, 1923. Protected by its case, this set is in excellent condition. £150-£200.

130 Victorian tray inkstand with taperstick, Henry Wilkinson, Sheffield, 1855. Although impressive in appearance, this piece is of poor quality, with stamped scroll decoration. £700-£1,000.

131 George III tray inkstand, Matthew Boulton, Birmingham, 1803, fitted with an inkwell, sander, wafer box, and taperstick with snuffer. £1,000-£1,500, as manufactured by a collected maker. Cheaper, Edwardian and later reproductions of this style are still readily available for £600-£800. *Photograph by courtesy of the Birmingham Assay Office.*

132 Edwardian copy of an eighteenth-century inkstand, by the Goldsmiths and Silversmiths Co. Ltd., London, 1918, with central baluster taperstick. £1,000-£1,200.

but larger specimens are usually expensive. Refinements, such as the addition of a wirework pen-rest soldered behind the lid or a pen-rest moulded into the front of the well, should enhance the value, as indeed will enamelled or tortoiseshell decoration.

Large, silver-mounted cut and moulded glass inkwells were also popular at the turn of the century. Many were six or more inches in diameter, with massive, heavy glass bodies and plain, hinged covers, sometimes inset with metal eight-day 'Goliath' pocket watches. Spiral-fluted specimens sell particularly well today, and the plain circular or square examples are also collected.

Most wooden dressing-cases were fitted with small silver travelling inkwells, often engraved with the initials or crest of their original owners. Eighteenth- and early nineteenth-century examples, whether square or circular, normally had small hinged covers. These screw down tightly with tiny nuts fitted with folding handles, to lie flush with the lid of the well when not in use. By the mid nineteenth century cylindrical specimens became popular. Their lids were furnished with bayonet fittings to ensure leak-proof closure. Leather dressing-cases also contained inkwells but these were usually made of chromium-plated steel.

Pens, Pencils, and Penknives

The quill dip pen has been in use for centuries, and special knives were developed to cut and shape the ends of the quills. These small, sharp penknives were similar in appearance to folding fruit knives (see chapter 2), although most had steel blades to carve the tough ends of the feathers into the requisite shapes. By the late eighteenth century the wealthy employed quill holders, usually made of carved wood, bone, or ivory. These followed the invention by Thomas Palmer of East Grinstead of a new system of cutting quill nibs to fit into a slender mount or holder.

The popularity of his novel idea led to Palmer being granted the Royal Warrant as pen-maker to His Royal Highness, King George III. Joseph Bramah developed the 'nib or slip pen contained in a wooden holder' even further. In 1809 he perfected a machine which would cut several nibs from one quill, making production both quicker and cheaper.

Although there had been several attempts to manufacture a more durable substitute for the natural quill in the late eighteenth century, none were successful. Joseph Gillott of Birmingham patented the first steel nib around 1820, and other makers soon followed his example. Few were able to satisfy the demand for an implement which would write smoothly, and most users found the new nibs scratchy and inflexible. Many firms continued to research the problem, the Edinburgh company Macniven and Cameron manufactured the celebrated 'Pickwick', the 'Owl', and the 'Waverley' pens, all of which were more successful in producing an even, smooth script. By the 1830s gold nibs were popular. Usually tipped with a tiny spot of iridium, the two metals combined to create a strong but flexible nib able to withstand 'the corrosive acids employed in the manufacture of ink'.

All these nibs required handles, and gold and silver nib holders made their appearance in the first quarter of the nineteenth century. Large numbers of these 'dip pens' are still available to the modern collector. Regrettably, they are rarely hallmarked and are therefore generally impossible to date with accuracy. One can still find 'dip pens' with bright-cut silver-mounted tortoiseshell, ivory, or mother-of-pearl handles. Some were made as tourist souvenirs, with the added novelty of a tiny peep-hole containing a view of any number of holiday resorts popular in the nineteenth century. Another type of novelty dip pen

133 Selection of dip pens and propelling pencils dating from 1882 to 1913, some by Mordan. Still inexpensive, their prices might range from £30-£60.

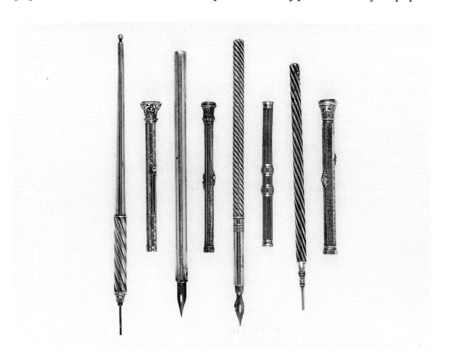

134 Two Mordan novelty pistol pencils. The larger, three inch example is made of silver, the smaller of nine carat gold decorated with rose diamonds and blue enamelling. Neither are hallmarked, although each is impressed with Mordan's name. Today the silver pencil would cost £200-£250, and the rarer gold example would retail for £400-£600.

135 Combination sealing wax holder and two pens, the latter designed to hold red and blue ink. These are indicated by the paste 'ruby' and 'sapphire' applied to each pen. Asprey, London, 1909, £100-£120.
Silver-overlaid vulcanite fountain pen c. 1920, the mount impressed 'Sterling'. Possibly American but no maker's mark. £70-£100.

made in the first half of the nineteenth century had a silver feather-shaped handle finely-engraved with barbs. Obviously a nostalgic and whimsical reference to the quill pens of the past, this variety is now much collected.

Although the fountain pen is thought to have been invented by Bramah in the early 1800s, these primitive forerunners of the modern pen were unsuccessful, leaking into pockets and producing blotches rather than elegant writing. The first fountain pen to pose a serious economic threat to the dip pen was the L. E. Waterman's 1884 model, made of vulcanite, with an internal reservoir and controlled flow. Other manufacturers based their designs firmly on that of Waterman, the American Caw's Safety Fountain Pen of the 1890s and Britain's Swan Pen, produced by Mabie, Todd, and Bard, and the Pelican Self-feeding Pen invented by De La Rue, using the same clumsy, messy method of filling the pen using a dropper with rubber bulb. Many efforts were made to overcome this problem, and in 1908 an American, W. A. Sheaffer patented the first pen filled by automatic lever action.

Many early fountain pens were advertised as 'leak-proof', but in fact, this was rarely the case. All manufacturers provided a closely-fitting sheath mount with lid as an extra safe-guard. This was often made of vulcanite decorated with marbling and overlaid with delicate silver or gold scrollwork. More expensive pens were entirely encased in silver or gold. Few of these pens were hallmarked, although American examples were frequently stamped 'sterling' or 'filled', the latter denoting the use of rolled gold or silver mounts covering a core of base metal. Old fountain pens have become popular and specialist shops have started up.

Just as an air of uncertainty surrounds much of the development of both dip and fountain pens, so the invention of the propelling pencil also remains shrouded in doubt. Sampson Mordan claimed that his former partner, John Isaac Hawkins, 'had invented or otherwise become possessed of the secret mystery and process of making and manufacturing certain Black Lead Pencil Points or Ever Pointed Pencils', this later sold to Mordan for £450 payable by installments. Certainly, an entry dated 1822 in the Patents' Office states: 'Hawkins and Mordan...for their invented improvements on pencil holders...for the purposes of facilitating writing and drawing by rendering the frequent cutting or mending of the points or nibs unneccessary'.

Joseph Willmore of Birmingham also made pencils, and in 1828 Mordan lodged a complaint, claiming that his own, patented, design had been copied by Willmore. Willmore denied the charge, and The Lord High Chancellor ruled in his favour, saying that there had been no infringement of patent rights. Other manufacturers took advantage of this decision to copy and improve Hawkins and Mordan's design, which led to further court cases. Perhaps we will never know who actually invented the propelling pencil. Nevertheless, the name most associated with their manufacture was, and still is, Sampson Mordan. Indeed, in the nineteenth century the word 'Mordan' was used as a synonym for 'pencil', the novelist Thackery writing; 'Tell me a curious anecdote or two, and write 'em off quickly, good Mordan, do!' Vast numbers, usually mounted in engine-turned silver or nine carat gold and often with a coloured glass or hard-stone seal terminal, were made throughout the century. Early examples were stamped S M G R. for Mordan and Riddle, but these are now quite rare, as the partnership was dissolved in 1837, when Mordan introduced his own individual punch. This can be seen on many pencils, some of which bear no other hallmarks. Later standard propelling pencils by Mordan are still quite inexpensive, likewise the pencil case, designed as a metal sheath to protect a single wooden pencil, can also be bought for very little. These were cheaper than Mordan's propelling pencils and seemed equally popular, and both types were still illustrated in the *Army and Navy Stores general price list of 1935-6*.

Sampson Mordan was equally well-known for his novelty propelling pencils, now extremely popular if in good condition. The earliest were probably the pistol and revolver varieties, dating from the 1850s. By the third quarter of the nineteenth century a large range of curiosities had been introduced, in the shape of frogs, pigs, owls, mussel shells,

136 Mordan novelty pencil formed as an owl, with staring yellow glass eyes. This piece is only two and a half inches long when fully extended. £200-£250.

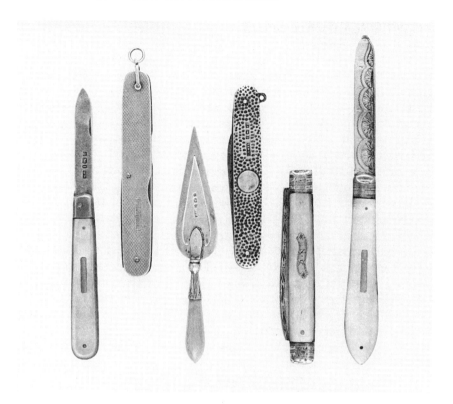

137 Collection of nineteenth- and twentieth-century pocket knives, the silver-bladed examples probably for fruit (see page 37), the steel-bladed knives for cutting quills. £30-£40 each. Edwardian trowel bookmark, Birmingham, 1901, with agate handle. £20-£40.

tennis rackets, cricket bats, lamps, and Egyptian mummies. Others incorporated paper knives, whistles, and penknives, and the standard propelling pencil was refined to include both nib and lead holders. Mordan even manufactured bi- and tri-coloured pencils with enamelled sliding bands, their colours indicating the lead contained within each section, and a special sketching set with five types of lead marked VH, H, M, S, and VS. The variations in hardness were designed for the amateur artist, who could now use one implement 'for all the purposes of fine outline and shading in pencil drawing'.

The firm continued to prosper well into the twentieth century, and production of pens, pencils, and other small novelties such as vesta cases and scent bottles continued throughout World War I, although the work-force was much depleted by conscription, and some space was devoted to valuable war work. After the war, the firm seemed to suffer from its policy: 'Quality lives when price is forgotten'. They continued to concentrate on well-made and therefore expensive objects, refusing to sacrifice quality while other firms produced cheaper, similar pieces to capture the middle-class market. The end finally came in 1941, when the factory was destroyed in a raid during the Blitz. The patents were bought by other pencil makers, finally ending up in the possession of The Yard-o-Led Pencil Company. The new owners decided that Mordan's designs were simply not economically viable for modern mass-production, and they disappeared into obscurity for many years, until rediscovered by recent collectors of small antique silver.

Tapersticks and Seals

In the early 1600s letters were usually sealed with coloured flour and gum wafers, at the time priced at one hundred for a penny. These, however, proved to be unreliable and so, by the late seventeenth century most people used melted wax, which was dripped onto the wafer to provide a more durable, secure seal. A further attraction of this method was that the warm, soft wax could be impressed with an intaglio carved with initials or a crest. One could then tell at a glance whether the letter had been tampered with, by examining the seal for any damage.

Sealing wax, a mixture of pure resin and colour, usually vermilion or lamp-black, could be bought in moulded blocks or in long strips. The latter was more convenient, as it incorporated a wick so that the flame necessary to melt the wax could be maintained. These strips were coiled around a pivoting silver rod turned by a handle, the end of the taper emerging through a pierced silver holder. While early wax-jacks had horizontal spindles, the eighteenth century saw the introduction of smaller jacks with vertical pivoting rods. Some are fitted with a circular holder split in the centre, to trap and hold the lit end of the taper securely. Here the two halves of the holder are operated with a sprung scissor-action to ensure a tight grip. More sophisticated examples were fitted with a wire spherical cage, serving to protect the ball of fragile wax. Most wax-jacks also had a tiny conical snuffer attached by a fine chain, the snuffer clipping into a little socket when not in use.

By the early eighteenth century cast baluster tapersticks had become popular. These were perfect miniature copies of contemporary

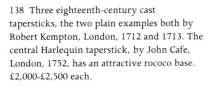

138 Three eighteenth-century cast tapersticks, the two plain examples both by Robert Kempton, London, 1712 and 1713. The central Harlequin taperstick, by John Cafe, London, 1752, has an attractive rococo base. £2,000-£2,500 each.

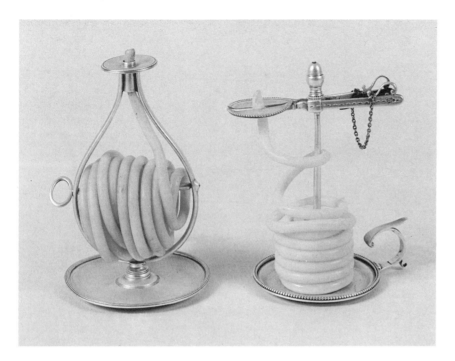

139 Two George III wax jacks: *left:* Peter and Ann Bateman, London, 1798, £800-£1,200; *right:* Samuel Herbert and Co., Sheffield, 1769; £800-£1,200.

candlesticks. Early examples had square, circular, hexagonal, or octagonal bases and simple waisted sockets, although mid eighteenth century fashions introduced gadrooning and fluting along with chased rococo decoration. Around 1760 the Corinthian column taperstick came into being, inspired by the architectural styles of Ancient Greece. A further much-loved style was the caryatid taperstick, possibly inspired by contemporary porcelain candlesticks. Here the flower-shaped nozzle is supported by a cast human figure, usually that of Harlequin or Columbine. Other types of caryatid tapersticks are known, and John Cafe, a specialist London candlestick maker, produced some fine examples with Chinaman and blackamoor stems. All cast eighteenth-century tapersticks are now very desirable, as their small size makes them ideal for modern dining rooms. Even copies of cast eighteenth-century tapersticks have become quite valuable as the antique specimens are now so expensive.

The third quarter of the eighteenth century saw the introduction of cheaper candle and tapersticks made from die-stamped thin sheet silver. These were normally strengthened by the insertion of an iron rod into the stem, the bases further weighted with pitch or plaster to create a false impression of solidity. These are justifiably less popular than their cast cousins, as their thin mounts are so often badly worn or split.

Throughout the eighteenth and nineteenth centuries, many inkstands were fitted with tapersticks, usually with flat square or circular bases applied with loop or scroll handles and thumb grips. Examples which have become detached from their inkstands can be recognized easily, as most specimens have a narrow silver band soldered onto the underside of their base. This originally fitted into a corresponding grove on the inkstand or into the wafer-box. Delicate flower and leaf-shaped

140 *Left:* die-stamped novelty taperstick by Joseph Willmore, 1831, typical of the inexpensive 'toys' mass-produced in Birmingham throughout the nineteenth century. £300-£400. *Photograph by courtesy of the Birmingham Assay Office.*

141 *Right:* George III travelling bougie-box, John Emes, London, 1804, applied with a loop handle and plain thumb-piece. Notice the pivoting crescent-shaped lid, designed to cut off the air supply, thereby extinguishing the flame. £300-£500.

142 Four Birmingham desk seals two and a half/three inches long, made in 1902, 1907, 1910, and 1913 respectively. All are quite flimsy, with machine-stamped, thin silver handles. Nevertheless, they are still popular today. £100-£120 each.

tapersticks made from die-stamped sheet silver were also introduced at this time, mostly produced in Birmingham. These pieces are generally of poor quality, yet their charm seems to outweigh their lack of strength and weight.

Sealing wax containers were also made for travelling purposes, serving as an essential tool for the eighteenth-century scribe called upon to assist those unable to write for themselves. These were called bougie boxes and most that survive date from the reign of George III, taking the form of a cylindrical box and cover. The cover is always pierced to allow the end of the wax coil to protrude. Larger bougie boxes often had an applied scroll handle and conical snuffer, attached by means of a fine chain. Pocket versions were more compact, their cut-out handles curved and hinged to lie flush with the side of the box, when not in use. Many small bougie boxes also had a pivoting cover to block off the hole in their lids. This cover also served as a snuffer. Both kinds of bougie box are generally plain, as they were designed to be functional. Some examples may be applied with reeding or beading or enlivened with bright-cut engraving, but this is unusual. Despite their lack of decoration they are popular today, many collectors admiring their simple and sturdy forms.

Once the sealing wax had been melted and dripped onto the letter or document, the writer would then add his personal mark, using a small metal, stone, or glass seal. Georgian fob seals are still readily available. Designed to hang from a watch chain or chatelaine, eighteenth-century examples were often made of silver, with plain oval base plates and delicate scroll handles, often pierced through by a tiny suspension loop. Few were fully hallmarked. Nineteenth-century fob seals were more ornate, their heavy silver-gilt or gilt brass mounts chased with flowers and foliage. Most were now inset with an intaglio, often made from foiled rock crystal, rose quartz, citrine or amethyst, or simply from brightly coloured glass.

Larger seals with sturdy handles were made for desk use; eighteenth-century examples normally had turned lignum vitae or fruitwood handles and silver intaglios. The nineteenth century saw the introduction of delightfully frivolous cast silver desk seals with figural handles, often formed as cherubs. More sedate specimens, designed for masculine use had grips in the shape of classical, biblical, or military figures. Cheaper versions were made from stamped metal and their handles often resembled those of shoe horns and button hooks (see chapter 5). Others were formed as a bird's claw, modelled as if tightly gripping a hardstone ball.

Silver sealing wax holders became popular at the end of the nineteenth century. These sometimes have a carved intaglio terminal similar to those found on contemporary pens and pencils. Many were fitted with a sliding mount, to eject the stick of wax as it burnt down. Wax holders were manufactured in large numbers by Mordan and his competitors, and retailed for a few shillings in the 1890s. Today they are still underpriced, providing the collector with an inexpensive and curious relic of the past.

Desk Bells and Candlesticks

While many desk accessories originated in the late nineteenth and early twentieth centuries, others have a much longer history. Table and desk bells date from the reign of George I and are of typical hand-bell form. Their handles, clappers, and bodies were all cast separately, each detachable piece bearing at least a lion passant punch. Although this simple shape was manufactured well into the nineteenth century, with copies still in production today, early British bells are quite rare. While many were made on the continent and in America, to summon the servants to the dining-room, English custom demanded that servants should stay throughout the meal. They served and cleared each course, and then

143 *Left* to *right:* Georgian bell by C.C., London, 1788, and a reproduction bell, Thomas Bradbury and Son, Sheffield, 1937. Both are cast, producing a satisfyingly rich sound, unlike their cheaper, die-stamped counterparts, £1,000–£1,200 and £400–£500; three twentieth-century bells: William Comyns, London, 1900, operated by twisting the button on the top, £200–£250; William Comyns, London, 1912, with glass body and thin stamped mounts, £200–£250; Elkington and Co, Birmingham, 1909, £600–£800.

144 Three pairs of dwarf candlesticks with short stems and loaded bases to ensure stability. Most examples were cheaply-made, with stamped mounts often badly worn with cleaning. *Left* to *right:* William Comyns, London, 1893, £200-£300; maker's mark rubbed, Birmingham, 1904, £150-£200; S.M.L. Ltd., Birmingham, 1936, £100-£150.

145 Amusing bell with key-wind action, operated by pressing the tortoise's tail. G.Y.and Co., Chester, 1912, £300-£400.

retired to stand against the walls, poised to deal with any problems, but discreetly out of earshot of the conversation. Some eighteenth-century inkstands were fitted with bells, but survivors are rare. As a result, Georgian cast hand-bells can sell for many hundreds of pounds. Victorian and Edwardian reproductions are more readily available to the collector, but these too are now quite expensive.

In the late nineteenth century novelty bells were introduced, including one amusing model of an old lady dressed in hooped skirts and swathed in shawls. As the bell rings her head nods vigorously, rather as if she is scolding a passer-by. Manufactured by Elkington and Co. of Birmingham, most examples of this type of bell were made of electroplate. Other Victorian bells were formed as tortoises, their clappers activated by depressing the tails. A spring mechanism wound by a concealed key produces a buzzing noise, simultaneously causing the animal's head to nod up and down. Such novelties appeal to the modern collector, and hallmarked examples in working order sell very well. Circular bells with pierced and stamped silver mounts are also popular. Operated by turning a central handle to activate the hammer-like clapper, they feel surprisingly heavy, the misleading weight provided by the plated bell rather than by the thin, delicate mount.

Obviously, in the days of flickering candle and gas-light, desks would need direct illumination, to avoid the dangers of eye-strain. Ordinary candlesticks could prove dangerous, toppling over quite easily to set the house on fire. This problem was of particular importance in the third quarter of the eighteenth century, when heavy, cast sticks were replaced by the lighter, filled variety. The silversmiths overcame the risk of fire to a certain extent, by introducing 'piano candlesticks', useful for desks, pianos, and any other unstable surfaces. This new form of stick had a large bottom and short column, and the weight was concentrated at the base to provide stability even while playing the most lively piano piece. The idea soon caught on, and many different styles were produced following current trends in fashion. To the modern eye, piano candlesticks may seem ugly, their overlarge bases and squat stems combining to create an unbalanced appearance. However, one is forced to admit that they function perfectly, providing a relatively safe method of casting light onto a writing surface.

At the turn of the century an even cheaper type of desk candlestick was produced in great quantity, also designed for stability, with the weight concentrated at the base. These so-called 'dwarf' candlesticks closely resembled the capstan inkwells (see page 108) in size, shape, and construction, and suffered the same risks of damage. They remained popular for many years and are therefore common today. Earlier specimens may be of slightly better quality, with spiral-fluted or guilloche-enamelled decoration, but all are inexpensive.

Photograph Frames, Blotters, and Stationery Boxes

Towards the end of the nineteenth century, when the photographic portrait became much cheaper and more readily available, the silver-mounted photograph frame came into its own. Every mantelpiece, piano, bookcase and desk was covered with a host of frames of all sizes. They were generally made from velvet and leather-covered wood applied with thin silver mounts. Today, after many years in the doldrums during the 1940s to the 1960s, when the sentimental clutter of Victoria's reign was regarded with derision, they are immensely popular.

From the 1880s until about 1915, most frames were smothered with exuberant decoration. Many are so ornate that the hallmarks are difficult to find. It usually helps if one checks the corners or the border of the cartouche first, as many are marked in these areas. These frames can be most attractive, their richly coloured, velvet backgrounds seen through the piercing, contrasting with the silver, to create a splendid impression using a minimal amount of the precious metal. Late Victorian frames varied tremendously in both shape and size. Oblong examples with arched tops with cartouches for initials, are the most common, but one can also find oval and circular frames. The most elaborate is the cartouche shape, its sides and top formed from asymmetrical scrolls and shells. This design was often reinforced by similar stamped decoration. The most prolific maker during the nineteenth and early twentieth centuries was undoubtedly William Comyns, a London silversmith specializing in inexpensive bibelots for the parlour and bedroom, who manufactured many thousands of pieces.

From about 1890 to 1910 Art Nouveau frames became popular, often decorated with spot-hammering to give a hand-made effect. Others were stamped with highly stylized flowers or with maidens with flowing

146 Typical turn-of-the-century frame with thin, stamped mount and velvet backing. Ten inches high. William Comyns, London, 1899, £250-£300.

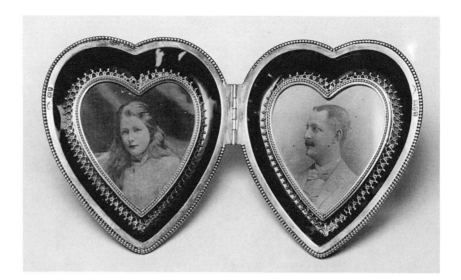

147 Victorian silver and tortoiseshell folding frame, by William Comyns, London, 1895, sold for £700 at auction in 1983. Heart-shaped objects are perennial favourites. £1,500-£2,000.

hair and robes, the latter closely resembling the subjects of many Pre-Raphaelite paintings. Specimens bearing the mark of Liberty and Co. will sell particularly well, as will some unusual frames stamped with old-fashioned and maudlin mottoes such as 'East, West, Home's Best' or 'Every Cloud has a Silver Lining'. Today these charming, mawkish sentiments seem to be much appreciated, judging from the high prices they invariably attract.

The 1920s and 1930s saw the introduction of a more severe photograph frame. Outlines became simple and decoration was either non-existent, or strictly limited to engine-turned line engraving. As the earlier styles of frame have shot up in value, so this type has followed, the new demand doubtless also stimulated by the current vogue for Art Deco design.

Miniature frames, often measuring no more than two inches in height, have always been popular. While some were simply smaller versions of the frames described above, others were of better quality, held upright by cast cherubs rather than by wooden easel supports. The collector may also come across two or more miniature frames joined with hinges to create a long folding strip. Alternatively, a large frame might have several small apertures to give an impressive group display. While most photograph frames were between six and twelve inches in height, some very large examples were also made, occasionally measuring as much as thirty-six inches in height. The latter are particularly popular as they can be converted into dressing-table mirrors.

However carefully one tries to clean silver photograph frames, it is inevitable that some of the polish will penetrate the pierced decoration, staining the velvet and leather mounts. Fortunately, the silver border mounts can be lifted off quite easily once the pins are removed, to enable the stained velvet background to be replaced. Such restoration will not have an adverse effect on the value, as long as one chooses the colours popular at the time when the frame was made. After all, it could well

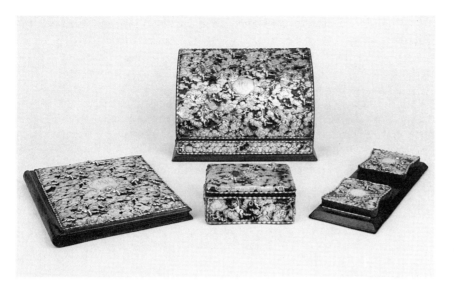

148 American late nineteenth-century desk set by Mauser, *c.* 1890, the mounts stamped and pierced with cherubs amidst clouds. Today it has become difficult to find a complete set, hence £800-£1,000.

have been recovered several times in the past. Suitable colours are deep crimson and purple, bottle green, and royal blue. One could, of course, try to match the original colour, or, less drastically, tint faded and stained frames with a felt-tip pen.

The collector must be aware of the many modern frames which have flooded onto the market over the last few years, manufactured using the same moulds and stamps and therefore almost identical to the originals. They have spread across the country, appearing regularly in many antique shops and markets and even in auction sales. It is not too difficult to spot these new frames, as their mounts lack the sharpness of the originals. All the decoration has a rounded, smooth appearance, due to the stamps themselves being worn with over-use.

Desk blotters were usually also applied with thin silver mounts. They were made in two forms, the first a large, flat folder designed for drying a whole letter, made from two sheets of leather-covered wood hinged together, each lined with blotting paper. The second variety of blotter, a smaller curved oblong with central handle, was used to dry a signature. Many blotters of both shapes were made of silver-mounted tortoiseshell, and these trinkets were highly prized during the late nineteenth century. *The Gentlewoman* of December 1892 comments: 'Quite the most delightful gifts would be some of the articles in tortoiseshell, these including a blotting-case of (sic) corners handsomely mounted in silver and a silver monogram in the centre'.

Silver-mounted stationery boxes are now quite expensive as they are large and impressive, with many examples measuring over twelve inches in length. Their curved, hinged covers open to reveal compartments lined in brightly-coloured moire silk, to match the leather exterior. Today one could expect to pay several hundreds of pounds for a perfect late Victorian or Edwardian stationery box, although the presence of a monogram or presentation inscription should reduce the value considerably.

Complete desk sets were common in the late nineteenth century, the wealthy supplying them in each guest bedroom. Apparently, hostesses despaired of the lively female visitor who required constant attention and entertainment, forcing the mistress of the house to neglect her duties. As a result, it would be casually suggested that each lady should retire to her room during the afternoon, ostensibly 'to write letters', the thoughtful hostess supplying the neccessary implements for this purpose. One can still occasionally find a complete desk set, with stationery box, one or both types of blotter, and an inkwell, but this has become increasingly difficult. Most have now been broken up, the individual pieces sold off separately for very little. Cheaper desk sets with capstan inkwells, candlesticks, and 'dip pens' were also sold at the turn of the century, their thin silver mounts usually protected by a fitted case. Inexpensive today, one could still find a complete, perfect set quite easily.

Clocks and Calendars

Desk clocks were made in large numbers throughout the second half of the nineteenth century. Many took the form of a miniature carriage clock with hinged carrying handle, based on the practical and sturdy travelling clocks made of brass originally used for carriage journeys. Silver desk examples are much smaller, few measuring more than three and a half inches from their tiny bun feet to the tops of their scroll handles. While most were simple in design and decoration, others were enhanced with enamelling or applied with hardstone or tortoiseshell plaques. These are particularly attractive, and command high prices today.

A second popular type of desk clock consisted of a large, silver-mounted rectangular wood and leather box containing a Goliath pocket watch, normally of base metal. In the nineteenth century the thin mounts were often ornately-pierced and stamped with foliage, birds, and masks, creating a rich and splendid impression from a small amount of silver. Many of these were made in the prolific workshop of silversmith William Comyns. Edwardian examples were usually much plainer, their mounts engine-turned with simple but effective lines. This type of desk clock was sometimes fitted with a battery and a tiny light bulb to illuminate the dial, presumably so that it could be used on a bedside table.

Silver-mounted clocks were also made for bedroom use. Many dressing table sets were provided with matching time-pieces, often folding into a compact, slim case when not in use. Popular in the 1920s and 1930s, they were usually decorated with coloured guilloche enamelling in attractive pastel shades. More striking examples were also made, with stylish Art Deco enamelling in strong and bright contrasting colours with angular zigzag designs.

Some mantel clocks used silver in their construction. Better quality examples were manufactured entirely from silver, but cheaper clocks

149 Nine study and bedroom clocks, mainly Edwardian, including two carriage clocks. The three examples on the right all contain metal eight-day Goliath pocket watches, while the clock top-left has a folding leather case and scroll-pierced silver mount. £300-£800.

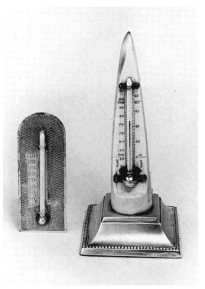

150 Two desk thermometers: *left* to *right:* simple engine-turned example, Walker and Hall, London, 1923, £100-£150; silver-mounted boar's tusk, Mappin and Webb, London, 1904, £120-£160.

151 Unusual combination clock and barometer made by William Comyns, London, 1900, £300-£350.

152 The above 'perpetual' desk calendars were made in London, in 1910, 1935, and 1922 respectively. Each has a thin silver mount, the central calendar decorated with engine-turning so typical of the Art Deco period. £100-£150.

were also made of oak or mahogany applied with thin, stamped metal mounts. Miniature versions were made of most of the shapes popular at the turn of the century, with Edwardian 'balloon' clocks and arched oblong examples still available in quite large numbers today.

Desk calendars were made in two main forms. The first was fitted with detachable celluloid squares painted with the days and months of the year. The date was altered by sorting through the tickets to find the right combination, and then displayed in a small silver holder mounted onto a pedestal foot. It is always wise to check that the tickets are complete. Any missing pieces would prove difficult to replace, thus rendering the calendar quite useless. The second type of calendar relied on information painted onto narrow linen strips wound through a system of cogs and rollers to reveal the relevant combination through an arrangement of small windows. These so-called 'perpetual' calendars were usually made of ebonized wood with stamped silver mounts, often decorated with engine-turning. Jammed rollers may well indicate that the linen strips have rotted or frayed, making the calendar an expensive 'white elephant' at any price.

Further Writing Relics

Letter-openers were produced in large numbers from the mid nineteenth century. Most had silver-mounted handles with stamped decoration, and with plain tortoiseshell or ivory blades. Examples made entirely from silver are unusual, and one must be aware of the conversion of Georgian meat skewers. Larger paper-knives were particularly fashionable at the turn of the century. Sometimes measuring fourteen to eighteen inches in length, their wide blades are now useless for opening letters, although they may well have been more practical for breaking seals, in the days

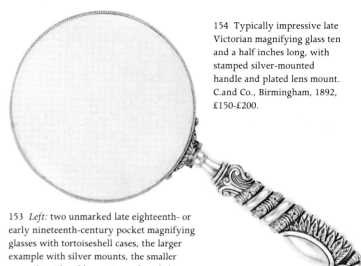

154 Typically impressive late Victorian magnifying glass ten and a half inches long, with stamped silver-mounted handle and plated lens mount. C. and Co., Birmingham, 1892, £150-£200.

153 *Left:* two unmarked late eighteenth- or early nineteenth-century pocket magnifying glasses with tortoiseshell cases, the larger example with silver mounts, the smaller example with gold mounts, and a gilt-brass quizzing-glass or lorgnette, *c.* 1830, £150-£200.

before the introduction of the gummed envelope. Certainly, the Victorians used them for cutting the pages of new books, but it seems likely that they were more decorative than functional. Some examples had curved elephant tusk handles applied with strapwork mounts, and specimens with scimiter-shaped tortoiseshell blades were also popular.

Both paper-knives and letter-openers in good condition are highly collected today, although their decorative value far outweighs any practical value, with the result that higher prices are usually asked for the larger, more impressive pieces. Tiny, trowel-shaped book-marks are also popular. Many have turned ivory or mother-of-pearl handles, or are applied with cast dogs' heads or game birds. Normally about two to three inches long, these small pieces sell very well today.

Desk magnifying glasses with embossed handles are not rare, but large and decorative examples are now expensive. The best specimens have applied cast mounts bordering the circular lens. There now seem to be a large number of magnifying glasses on the market made up from new lenses with plated mounts. These have handles created from antique silver knife handles removed from broken or worn knives and then glued onto the lens mount. Made up magnifying glasses should be far less expensive than their original counterparts, providing a cheap yet handsome alternative.

Pocket magnifying glasses are also quite common. They have gold or silver mounts, and the fragile glass lens pivots to fit inside a tortoiseshell or mother-of-pearl cover when not in use. Although few specimens were hallmarked, their shell and foliate mounts and crude pinning suggests manufacture in the eighteenth and early nineteenth centuries.

Stamp boxes became an essential part of desk equipment after the introduction of the penny post in 1840, although early examples are very rare. Presumably, most people used the wafer-boxes on their inkstands for storing stamps during the mid nineteenth century, and most surviv-

155 This wonderful combination paperweight and sander was made by Thomas William Dee, London 1862. £1,500-£2,000.

156 Novelty double letters clip on leather-covered base, the clips themselves applied with a cast terrier tormenting a spitting cat. Made by T.D. and W.D., London, 1892, it is typical of the Victorian taste for the whimsical. £600-£800.

157 Edwardian double stamp box applied with scrolls, the lid inset with two genuine but badly faded stamps. Made in London, 1904, it has an indeciferable maker's mark. £150-£200.

158 Three inexpensive paper knives, one with a pair of matching silver-handled scissors in a leather case applied with initials. *Top* to *bottom*: Maker's mark rubbed, Sheffield, 1896, £250-£300 the set; Sampson Mordan and Co., London, 1896, combination pencil and paper knife, £200-£250; Asprey's, London, 1906, combination magnifying glass and paper knife, £150-£200.

ing stamp boxes date from the turn of the century. Today they are immensely popular, doubtless because British stamps have remained at the same size. Many are inset with a genuine stamp in a tiny glazed frame, although these stamps may be faded from long exposure to sunlight. Tiny envelopes were also made for a single stamp. These had suspension loops, so that they could hang from a gentleman's fob chain. Plain examples are quite inexpensive, as they are less popular than their desk equivalents. Some specimens were far more elaborate however, manufactured as facsimiles of real envelopes, with engraved names and addresses and tiny enamelled stamps and postmarks. These are far more popular, their novelty value much appreciated by modern collectors who are willing to pay high prices for examples in good condition.

The users of dip pens with steel nibs were beset with constant problems, as the ends of the nibs became clogged with old ink. Steel nibs had to be cleaned regularly by wiping with a brush with stiff bristles, usually resembling a miniature scrubbing brush. In wealthy households these were often mounted in silver. Amusing specimens might be formed as pigs or chickens, or, more appropriately, as porcupines or hedgehogs, the bristles of the brush forming the animal's spines.

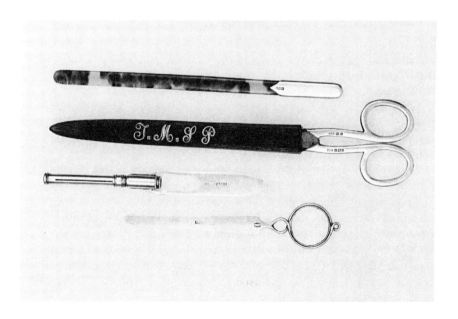

7 The Tobacco Trade

Pipes, Tampers, and Tobacco Boxes and Jars

The first European to be credited with the discovery of tobacco was Columbus, who landed in the Bahamas in 1492. More interested in precious stones and metals, his followers simply threw away the first dried tobacco leaves exchanged by the Indians for cheaply produced European goods. Eventually, one member of the crew must have decided to try the curious custom of inhaling smoke from smouldering leaves, and his habit soon caught on, certainly reaching Britain by the mid sixteenth century. One of the first reports of smoking here was that of a sailor who was attacked by a mob in Bristol, in 1556, and who narrowly escaped being stoned to death. His 'crime' of 'emitting smoke from his nostrils' first terrified, and then enraged the local populace, who believed that he was the Devil incarnate.

Tobacco soon became a luxury commodity, as the risks associated with its importation ensured high prices. It was enjoyed as an expensive delicacy in the most elevated circles, and was probably introduced to the English court by the explorer Hawkins, in the 1570s. European consumption of tobacco predates that in Britain by some twenty years, and, in 1559, the French Ambassador to the Portuguese court carried a quantity, with full and detailed instructions for its use and enjoyment, as a valuable and important gift to Catherine de Medici.

Ironically, smoking was encouraged as a health-giving pastime. The writer Thevet, in 1558, described it as 'very good for loosening and carrying off the superfluous humours of the brain', and it was actually believed to be a cure for cancer! It was soon established that no medical benefits accompanied its inhalation, and later writers began to condemn tobacco. Henry Buttes claimed it 'mortifieth and benummeth; causeth drowsiness; troubleth and dulleth the senses', and Joshua Sylvester, Court Poet to James I, described tobacco as: 'hell dust, England's shame, a madness, a frenzy, that by the devil's agency has been brought from savages to England'. Royalty had begun to disapprove, and Elizabeth I issued a decree, in 1584, deploring the use of tobacco. James I was another outspoken critic, publishing his famous pamphlet: *Counterblaste to Tobacco*, in 1604. A shrewd monarch, he also took advantage of his

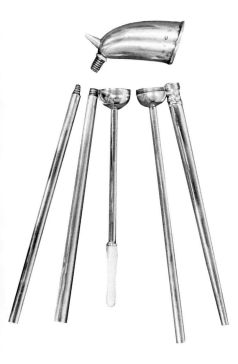

159 George III 'churchwarden' pipe with dismountable stem and ivory mouthpiece, Joseph Taylor, Birmingham, 1811. This presentation pipe was originally given to one of the Presidents of the 'Smoking Society' founded in 1790. £600-£800. *Photograph by courtesy of the Birmingham Assay Office.*

subjects' weakness to supplement the state's income, by raising the tax on tobacco from two pence to six shillings and ten pence per pound, a rise of 4,000 percent! Neither the pamphlet, nor the less subtle vast increase in price did much to stem the tide, and it is estimated that, by 1614, there were over 7,000 retail tobacconists in London alone.

Silver was rarely used for pipes, as the metal would quickly become too hot to hold in comfort. Most pipes were made from carved stone or wood, or from moulded clay, but the most elaborate examples had silver mounts, and were sometimes studded with precious stones. Many had pierced hinged lids to act as wind shields, so that the pipe could be used in the open air, and they were often fitted with amber mouthpieces, to ensure that the smoke was cooled before inhalation.

The majority of people used long, fragile church-warden pipes made of unglazed clay, often measuring over one foot in length. They were occasionally made in silver in the late eighteenth century, their long stems unscrewing into several more manageable sections for ease of transport. These were almost certainly presentation pieces, designed for show rather than for use, and consequently a fair number of examples have survived. In America silver pipes were produced as gifts to placate Indian chieftains, along with medals, bracelets, and gorgets, or chest plates. All are now extremely rare.

In the early eighteenth century meerschaum (magnesium silicate) was introduced from the Continent. Meerschaum lent itself to fine and elaborate carving. It also carbonizes as it absorbs nicotine, gradually changing in colour from creamy white to a rich nutty brown. Many examples have silver mounts joining the bowls to the amber mouthpieces. Eighteenth-century pipes are now rare, and the majority of specimens found today will date from the 1880-1920 period, when pipe-smoking underwent a revival. Silver-mounted briar pipes were introduced in the nineteenth century, and may still be found in their fitted

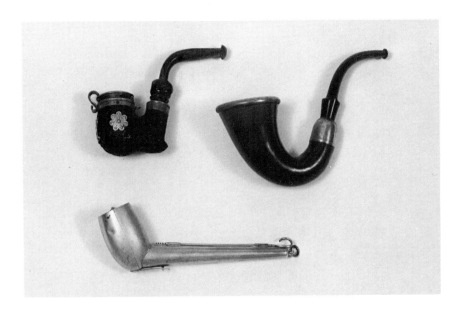

160 Two silver-mounted pipes: an unmarked, carved wood example, and a meerschaum example, A.B. Ltd., Birmingham, 1907. Notice that the first pipe has a hinged 'wind-shield' cover. £100-£120 each. Beneath them is a rare Victorian pipe case with detachable pricker, S.and S., Edinburgh, 1880, £120-£160.

161 Three tobacco boxes: *left* to *right:* C.F., London, 1803, engraved: 'Faithful to his Friend and Trust', £300-£400; C.D., London, 1923, decorated with engine-turning, £150-£200; unmarked silver and tortoiseshell, with inscription dated 1722, £300-£400.

cases, in almost pristine condition. Although normally inexpensive, examples with deeply-curved bowls are more collected, no doubt because of their association with the fictional detective, Sherlock Holmes.

Pipe tampers, used to pack the tobacco down into the bowl of the pipe, were normally made of brass, or of carved wood, bone or ivory. Silver pipe tampers are very rare, and can easily be confused with the more common desk seal (see chapter 6). The latter would normally have initials, a crest or a motto deeply engraved into the seal, this creating the impression in the hot wax. Pipe tampers, on the other hand, had plain, flattened terminals, with any decoration concentrated onto the handle.

Early tobacco boxes in silver are rare, although examples in brass and fused plate can be found easily. One can only assume that silver specimens were melted down when pipe-smoking became unfashionable, the cheaper boxes surviving in far larger quantities as the materials used in their manufacture were of such small intrinsic value. Tobacco boxes were oval or oblong in shape, differing from contemporary snuff boxes in size alone, with examples often measuring four to six inches. Most were quite plain, although primitive floral and foliate engraved designs have been noted. The majority were of sturdy construction, their makers using heavy gauge metal to create substantial and weighty boxes. While seventeenth-century examples are rare, there are far more eighteenth- and nineteenth-century specimens available to the collector, normally made in Holland or Germany. Their decoration ranges from simple engine-turning to elaborately hand-chased rural and bucolic scenes, often adapted from Dutch seventeenth-century oil paintings.

The late nineteenth century saw the introduction of the tobacco 'pebble', a small flattened oval or circular box designed to fit easily into the pocket. These were normally completely smooth, with flat hinges and no projecting lip to open the lid, which was released by compressing the sides to spring the catch. Most examples are now rather battered, with loose lids and deformed hinges, so perfect specimens have become quite expensive.

While most pipe-smokers carried their tobacco in small, air-tight boxes, designed to fit snugly into the pocket, larger supplies were also kept at home. These were stored in jars of pottery or lead-lined wood, and occasionally the collector may find an example with plain silver mounts, the hallmarks indicating manufacture in the late nineteenth or

162 Electro-plated tobacco jar and cover decorated with a frieze of seventeenth-century figures, Elkington and Co., Birmingham, *c.* 1880, £150-£200.

early twentieth century. Such tobacco jars were popular birthday and Christmas presents, and were often depicted in advertisements in the *Illustrated London News*, a magazine widely-read some eighty years ago. Some '*de luxe*' versions had silver clamps on their lids, which screwed down tightly to ensure that the tobacco maintained its moist freshness, and there were many novelty examples with crossed pipes in silver forming the handle, and the word 'tobacco' applied to the jar itself, so that no-one could mistake the function of the piece. Tobacco jars are popular today, particularly if the body was made by a well-known and collected pottery manufacturer such as Royal Doulton. Examples made by this company were usually of a simple barrel shape glazed in a rich treacle brown.

Snuff Boxes

163 Early American and British snuff boxes are very similar in both shape and decoration. The former are much rarer however. The above example was made by Bartholomew Schaats of New York, *c.* 1720, and is just under three inches long. £4,000-£6,000.

The consumption of tobacco in the form of powdered snuff was introduced to Britain from France in the early 1600s, and before long an elaborate ritual became established. This was a curious combination of gracefulness, politeness and practicality. Once again, it was hoped that tobacco in the form of snuff would conquer a multitude of ailments, ranging from migraine to the plague, and by 1640 pipe-smoking had been largely superseded amongst the upper classes. It reappeared in the mid nineteenth century, with a new-found respectability.

The earliest snuff boxes were simple and very plain. The only decoration to be found was primitive engraving, usually of scrolling foliage and flowers, and often incorporating the original owner's crest or initials. Although very small, usually measuring no more than one and a half inches in length, these boxes are remarkably sturdy, and can be found in excellent condition. Many had gilt interiors to prevent the snuff from corroding the silver. The most popular shape was a simple oval, often with flattened ends for ease of handling, but circular examples can be found, although these are much rarer. Early seventeenth-century snuff boxes are expensive today, although few are fully marked.

As the seventeenth century progressed, the taking of snuff became increasingly widespread despite the ridicule of influential writers. In the *London Spy*, published in 1690, Ned Ward wrote: 'We squeezed through a Fluttering Assembly of Snuffing Peripatetics − the Clashing of their Snuffbox lids, in opening and closing, made more noise than their Tongues and sounded as Terrible in my Ears as the Melancholy Ticks of so many Death Watches. . .'. Other writers claimed that, at church, they could not hear the sermon, the priest's voice totally drowned by the noises of the snuff-takers, as they first tapped the lids of their boxes, to dislodge any loose grains, followed by the loud 'sniffs' of inhalation, and finally the inevitable sneezes. Ladies who took snuff were particularly scorned, with complaints that even the strongest perfumes could not disguise the ever-present pungent tobacco odour. Others argued that the traditional skills of women, such as needlework and cooking, were now suffering as snuff-taking became associated with relaxation. Despite these criticisms, women continued to indulge in snuff for many years. In fact, as late as 1780 many ladies had special pockets sewn inside their gowns, to hold the dainty snuff boxes close to the warmth of their bodies. This gentle heat was supposed to bring out the aromatic bouquet of the snuff.

Toward the end of the seventeenth century silver was often combined with other materials such as ivory, tortoiseshell and mother-of-pearl, often decorated with piqué-work shells and scrolls. More elaborate shapes became popular, including the shell, the cartouche and the shaped oblong. This type of box was made for some seventy years, from the 1690s to the 1760s. Occasionally a date may be included in the piqué decoration but this is rare, and would consequently double or even treble the price.

By the middle of the eighteenth century cartouche-shaped boxes inset with Scottish agates or Derbyshire fluorspars became fashionable, their mounts often beautifully chased with rococo flowers and cherubs. Even 'Parrot or Cannel coal', polished to a marble-like finish, was used by the silversmiths, constantly striving to create novelty designs for the discerning customer. Boxes were now often two and a half to three and a half inches long, becoming great status symbols for the wealthy. Some people had many different boxes, often studded with precious stones or delicately painted with enamels, and dandies were said to have matching snuff boxes and clothes, with elaborate examples to accompany evening wear and more prosaic specimens for daytime use.

By the 1770s, new techniques in mechanical rolling ensured a plentiful supply of inexpensive, thin sheet silver, and snuff boxes became readily available to the middle classes at much lower prices. The inven-

164 Three 'castle top' boxes by Nathaniel Mills of Birmingham, made in the 1830s. Examples with sharp decoration are now expensive, and there may be a premium on those which depict unusual landmarks. The large table snuff box cast with a hunting scene would sell very well today. £400-£800.

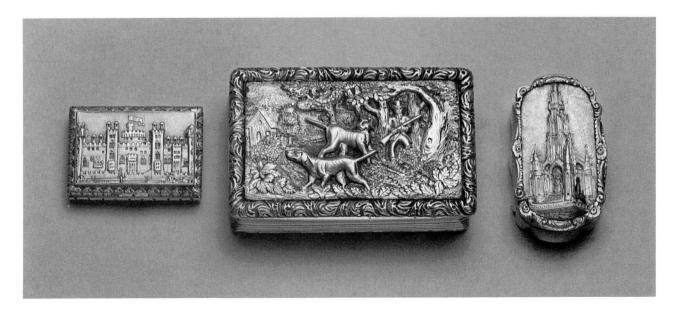

165 Four standard Birmingham mid nineteenth-century snuff boxes with machine-engraving, each with an inscription or monogram. £150-£200 each.

tive 'toy-makers' of Birmingham produced many thousands of snuff boxes and other gewgaws, examples of which are still inexpensive today. By now, the manufacturers of fused plate were producing even cheaper wares, their circular or oval snuff boxes inset with tortoiseshell or die-stamped with attractive rococo designs. To combat this competition, the Birmingham silversmiths introduced new patterns such as the octagon and the navette, or boat shape. These designs were chosen deliberately for their angles, and were impossible to copy in plate as each join would reveal the tell-tale evidence of copper at the corner, difficult to conceal without the use of ugly strips of silver. Many specimens were decorated with bright-cut engraving, giving a sparkling effect, with charming floral designs or naive hunting and shooting vignettes, the latter often derived from the wood-cuts of Thomas Bewick. Once again, this style of decoration was impossible on early plated boxes.

At the turn of the eighteenth century, snuff boxes became larger, with oblong examples sometimes measuring three and a half to four and a half inches in length. Such examples are generally sold today as 'table snuff boxes', and are thought to have been used after dinner, the host supplying his guests with snuff after the gentlemen had withdrawn to the library. Certainly, they are often very heavy, and would probably have been uncomfortable to carry. Smaller pocket boxes were often decorated with engine-turned engraving, which served to conceal the inevitable scratches caused by frequent handling, or by contact with coins and other oddments kept in the same pocket. Better quality snuff boxes had applied cast mounts and thumb-pieces, often chased with shells and flowers, and many examples were made with applied plates on their hinged lids, these decorated with hunting or battle scenes, or with religious or classical motives. Sporting designs are the most popular today, with early boxing or cricketing subjects priced well beyond the reach of most collectors.

At the beginning of the nineteenth century, snuff-taking was perhaps at its peak, and establishments such as Fribourg and Treyer of The Haymarket kept at least fifty varieties of snuff in stock, as well as creating new blends for special customers. Snuff boxes became increasingly attractive, and many novelty examples were made by the craftsmen of both Birmingham and London. One of the most important makers at this time was Nathaniel Mills of Birmingham, who produced fox and eagle head boxes with crisp, realistic fur and feather chasing. Although many of his contemporaries were equally talented, none seem to attract the same interest today, and pieces by Mills will always cost at least twice as much as examples by other, less collected silversmiths.

The early nineteenth century also saw the introduction of the 'castle-top' box, with its cast view of a building in high relief. Many famous landmarks were celebrated in this way, with views of Windsor Castle, Westminster Abbey and York Minster being among the most common. Rarities include various university colleges, Birmingham town hall and the Norwich corn exchange. Numerous examples were made of unidentifiable castles and cathedrals, the designs generally taken from contemporary engravings. Although the best 'castle-tops' were cast, other cheaper versions were made with die-stamped designs. Hardened steel dies were chased with patterns and then stamped into the much softer silver, using steam-driven presses capable of exerting tremendous pressure. Many copies could be made before the steel die lost its sharpness, and each piece of silver required very little hand finishing to produce a convincing copy of an individually cast and subsequently more expensive snuff box lid. Today all 'castle-tops' are much collected, particularly if the design is still sharp and crisp. The heavier cast examples should normally cost twice as much as die-stamped specimens.

By the 1830s fashions were beginning to change, with the introduction of cigars from America and the Continent. As if to hasten the decline of snuff-taking, a Professor Uyr published a widely-read report which stated that most snuff contained: 'Starch, cereals, sawdust, ground glass, lead oxide and milled sienna and rhubarb leaves coloured with burnt sienna and yellow ochre and made pungent with ammonia'. Modish people no longer indulged, and in 1835 snuff-taking was described, in *Hints on Etiquette*, as 'an idle, dirty habit, practised by stupid people in the unavailing endeavour to clear their stolid intellect . . . An élégant cannot take snuff without decidedly losing caste'. This gradual demise was hastened when both Queen Victoria and the Duke of Wellington condemned the habit in public. Such distinguished opinions could not be ignored, and by the mid nineteenth century snuff-taking had become a much despised and old-fashioned pastime. Although lingering in a few male bastions, the heyday of the silver snuff box was now over, with very few examples displayed at The Great Exhibition of 1851.

Snuff Mulls and Spoons

In Scotland, snuff mulls (the word probably derives from snuff mill) were popular. They were made from silver-mounted horns, sea shells, and even tiny, complete tortoise shells, their hinged covers often inset with plaques of polished rock crystal, smoky quartz, and other semi-precious stones indigenous to Scotland. The stones were often foiled with shiny paper to add both brilliance, and a richer colour. Most examples were unmarked, or simply bore the initials of the maker. They seem to have been made from the late 1600s to the nineteenth century, with little change in style to aid the collector in identification or dating. Some specimens do have presentation inscriptions however, often incorporating a date to commemorate a specific event. Others were given as prizes for horse races, Highland games, and agricultural shows.

Shell snuff mulls were usually made from exotic cowrie shells, a shape which lent itself to the creation of containers for powdered snuff. Most have flat silver lids hinged at the blunt end of the shell, although rarer examples can be found, where the sides of the shell near the opening have been mounted with sturdy hinges, to form the cover. Sometimes, mussel shells were used, although the end result must have been rather unsatisfactory, these shells being too shallow to contain very much snuff.

The horn used for the manufacture of snuff mulls had to be boiled for several hours, until soft and pliable. Once this stage was reached, the horn was coiled around a stick, to make a compact shape to fit inside the pocket. Tightly-bound, it was then allowed to cool, maintaining its shape as it hardened until ready to be cut and polished, before the silver mounts were applied. Many had thistle decoration incorporated into their mounts and hinges, and smaller examples were often given chains and finger rings, so that ladies could carry them with ease. Larger horn snuff mulls for table use were also made, especially in the late eighteenth and early nineteenth centuries, often with several appendages attached with fine chains to the mull. These 'tools' might include tiny ivory or bone hammers to break up caked snuff, rakes, to extract any impurities, and even brushes, which were used by the fastidious to remove loose snuff from the upper lip and moustache. Preserved hares' feet were used for this purpose, their grisly, mummified remains still sometimes attached to a table snuff mull. The larger, table mulls seem to be less popular than the pocket version, despite their greater rarity and more impressive size.

166 Two unmarked late eighteenth- or early nineteenth-century pocket mulls made from a polished tree root and a seashell, and a Victorian snuff box, the lid and base made from sections of elephant's molar, C.R., London, 1839. Many natural materials were exploited by silversmiths to create novelty boxes for their customers. £200-£400.

167 Three unmarked early eighteenth-century tortoiseshell snuff boxes inlaid with silver and gold wirework decoration. £300-£400 each.

168 Victorian ram's head snuff mull on wheels, with thistle mounts applied to the tips of the horns. R.and H. B. Kirkwood, Edinburgh, 1885, £3,000-£4,000.

169 Victorian single horn mull, the hinged cover inset with a foiled amethyst, C.B.S., Edinburgh, 1878, £600-£800.

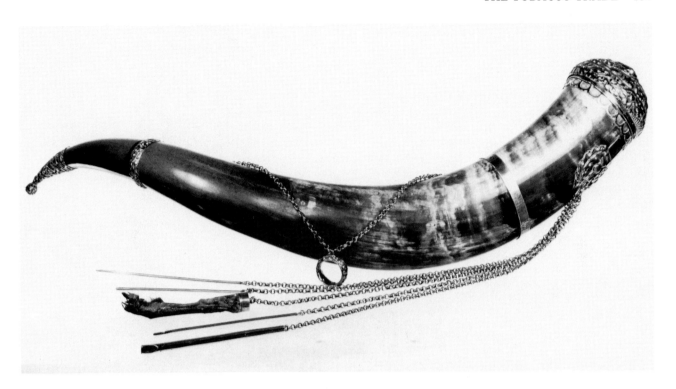

170 George IV mull complete with attachments, including a shrivelled hare's foot moustache brush. The mull is made from a polished ox horn instead of the more standard ram's horn. A.H., London, 1827, £600–£800.

In the mid nineteenth century, massive table snuff mulls were made from stuffed and mounted rams' heads. These beasts were bred especially for this purpose on the Scottish islands, each creature tethered at a safe distance from its neighbour to avoid the risk of confrontation, with the subsequent inevitable damage to their splendid, elaborately-curling horns. Many were mounted onto ivory wheels, so that they could be pushed and pulled along the massive Victorian dining tables, and Scottish decoration was again a popular feature, tiny thistle heads even applied to the tips of the horns. Although these snuff mulls were undoubtedly made primarily for show, they did, of course, include a snuff box, which was usually let into the centre of the head or into the muzzle. Many examples also had the appendages already described, hanging from little hooks fastened to the snuff box itself. Interestingly, while snuff-taking was generally regarded as a disgusting habit in the mid nineteenth century, these rather grotesque mulls were made well into the Edwardian era, largely for regimental or masonic use, and to grace the tables of gentlemen's clubs.

While most snuff-users simply helped themselves to a pinch of snuff, the more elegant used tiny spoons made of extremely thin silver. These were only two to two and a half inches in length, and usually bore only a maker's mark, generally struck low down on the stem near the back of the bowl. Many were originally stored in etuis, along with other fittings (see chapter 8), this protection ensuring survival despite their great fragility. Snuff spoons were made in all of the flatware patterns of the first half of the eighteenth century, the most common examples today being those of Hanoverian pattern.

Cheroot and Cigarette Accessories

Cheroots were introduced from America and the Continent in the 1830s, rapidly overtaking snuff in popularity, although Queen Victoria apparently disapproved of smoking. Her unfortunate guests at Balmoral would stand in the fire-places of their bedrooms, blowing cigar smoke up the chimney in an attempt to escape detection, but the Queen invariably caught the culprits, scolding them severely however elevated their rank in society.

Cheroot or cigar cases were made in silver and silver-mounted leather and crocodile skin, and were usually designed to hold three to five cigars, although torpedo-shaped cases were also made for individual smokes. Many were curved to fit snugly into the pocket. Plain, engine-turned and foliate bright-cut examples are quite common, but the most expensive are those with enamelled scenes, especially if these are of an erotic nature. As with vesta cases, many plain examples have been

171 Selection of inexpensive turn-of-the-century cigarette cases, one of them enamelled to simulate shagreen. £30-£70.

172 While plain cigarette cases sell badly today, enamelled specimens are much collected, particularly if decorated with erotic scenes or animals. *Left:* Sampson Mordan and Co., London, 1893, £600-£800; *right:* German low-grade silver *c.* 1890, £700-£1,000.

173 Cheroot case decorated with a splendid, saucy 'Gaiety Girl' made by George Heath, London, 1888, £600-£800.

enamelled recently, but they can be detected with ease by the discerning collector.

When cigarettes appeared, in the late nineteenth century, the silversmiths wasted little time, producing miniature cheroot cases in silver and gold to cater for the new demand. Today these are generally not very saleable, despite the excellent manufacture of their tiny hinges and catches. Nowadays fewer and fewer people smoke, and moreover, the modern king size cigarette is too large to fit most old cases, hence the current neglect of these pieces. Pretty examples can be used as card cases, but most sell at auction for their bullion value, and are generally melted down for scrap. Enamelled examples are surprisingly in demand, in spite of their complete uselessness, although only the unusual sell really well. There are many Art Deco specimens to be found in both auction houses and antique shops, normally guilloche-enamelled in bright colours. Monochrome examples are particularly common, and so fare badly, their price usually fixed at some twenty percent above the current scrap value of the metal. Multi-coloured examples in strong geometric designs are far more popular.

Minaudieres were made from the beginning of the twentieth century, to hold cigarettes along with lighters, powder compacts, lipstick holders, and mirrors. Many had leather, kid, or embroidered outer covers with strap handles, as they were used as evening bags, containing everything a fashionable woman might need.

Cigar and cigarette boxes, normally lined in cedar wood to prevent the tobacco from drying out, are commonly available, although many of the survivors are in poor condition. Large humidors or cigar boxes are quite expensive, but cigarette boxes are little collected, perhaps due to the decline in smoking in recent years. While most cigar and cigarette

174 Cheroot cases are more popular than cigarette cases. These three examples were all made in Birmingham at the end of the nineteenth century. £150-£200 each.

175 Although most table cigarette boxes are still quite cheap, pieces made by Ramsden and Carr are far more popular. Usually made in the Arts and Crafts style of the 1880s, with hammered designs and applied enamelled plaques, they were, in fact, manufactured in the first quarter of this century. £1,000-£1,500.

176 One may be lucky enough to find a case with lighter in unused condition, the enamel still perfect half a century after it was made. This set, by Mappin and Webb, Sheffield 1932, would now sell for £200-£300, a low price as the subject chosen by the artist is rather dull.

177 Art Deco minaudières are very popular if in perfect condition. The above specimen, made in 1932 and retailed by Dunhills, includes a watch and a lipstick holder, as well as the more standard cigarette case and lighter. £800-£1,000.

178 Victorian table cigar cutter, Joseph Braham, London, 1898. The inscription would deter most collectors, so this piece might cost £100-£120. A plain example would retail for £200-£250.

boxes are plain, or have simple engine-turned decoration, others are stamped with rococo flowers or foliage. Better quality examples were made by Omar Ramsden and Alwyn Carr, using much thicker silver, generally with spot-hammered decoration. Many were also applied with twisted wire mounts and inset with enamelled plaques, usually in the typical green, blue and brown shades so popular in the Art Nouveau period. These pieces by Ramsden and Carr are now very expensive.

In the 1930s cigarettes were also kept in canisters shaped rather like small tea-caddies. Once again lined with cedar, they are often decorated with engine-turning or spot hammering. Some even have a novelty action upon opening, an interior mechanism fanning out and displaying the cigarettes, each in an individual holder. The price of such pieces is much influenced by the current fashion for Art Deco.

Cigar cutters and piercers were normally made of steel, although many had plain or engine-turned silver mounts, often engraved with crests or initials. Mainly manufactured from the Edwardian period onwards, they are still readily available. The small version was originally designed to hang from a watch chain, and was therefore fitted with a tiny suspension loop, still useful as it enables the cutter to be attached to a key-ring. Larger, table or desk top cigar cutters are more unusual. Generally five to seven inches long, and often heavy enough to act as a paper-weight, they can now be expensive if in good condition.

Cigar and cigarette holders were popular from the late nineteenth century, and can still be found in large numbers today. Mostly made of pressed amber with nine carat gold mounts, each had its own tapering silver case, again usually with suspension loop. In the 1920s long cigarette holders became fashionable, many with engine-turned mounts and plastic mouthpieces. One may occasionally be lucky enough to find a stylish Art Deco set with six or more interchangeable mouthpieces in different colours, presumably to match the user's ensemble. A set retailed by Dunhills recently sold for £110 at auction.

Vesta Cases, Lighters, and Smokers' Companions

Although early smokers had to rely on base metal tinder boxes to obtain a flame, 'vestas' were introduced in the nineteenth century. These were made from thick cotton threads dipped in paraffin wax, the phosphorus heads igniting when rubbed against roughened serrations. Small oblong vesta cases were made, many with tiny loops to suspend the box from a watch-chain, and silversmiths soon found that the plain surfaces lent themselves to various styles of decoration. Known as 'match safes' in America, they are commonly engine-turned, bright-cut with flowers and leaves, or stamped with rococo scrolls or shell fluting. The most collected vesta cases today are those decorated with enamelling. Subjects vary tremendously, with mildly erotic scenes the most expensive, closely followed by animals, sporting pictures, and those displaying appallingly bad puns. Many were made to resemble visiting cards or envelopes, the latter with minute stamps and postmarks executed in brightly coloured enamel.

As enamelled vesta cases are now very costly, it is hardly surprising that many plain examples have been decorated recently, in an attempt to entrap the unwary buyer. In fact, the enamelling itself must always be examined with great care, as genuine examples are always covered with a network of tiny scratches, often visible only with the aid of a magnifying glass. The colours should be bright and clear, with a certain subtlety. The image itself, whatever the subject, will always be well-painted, with much attention to detail. Modern pieces are comparatively crude, with poor, clumsy designs, strident colours, and a rather 'muddy' appearance, particularly in the darker brown, green and blue tones. More obviously, they appear to be brand-new, with none of that surface scratching caused by contact with watches or coins in pockets over many years of use. Some vesta cases are even decorated with plastic 'enamelling', detected by tapping gently with a coin. Genuine enamel produces a

179 Unusual Victorian table lighter formed as Mr Punch, maker's mark rubbed, London, 1882, £800-£1,000.

180 Selection of turn-of-the-century table lighters, *left* to *right:* Roman lamp type, Walker and Hall, Sheffield, 1914, £100-£150; Grenade or bomb type, Mappin Brothers, Sheffield, 1903, £100-£150; Vase shape, C. and B., London, 1912, £100-£150.

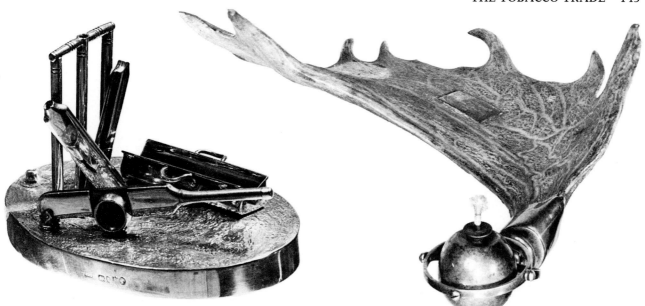

181 'Cricketiana' is now extremely popular, and collectors will pay extraordinarily high prices for antiques with a cricketing theme. This smoker's companion, made in London, 1895, includes a lighter, a vesta box, and a cigar cutter. £1,000–£1,500.

182 American lighter with elk antler handle, the weighted spherical lighter mounted on a gimbel. Impressed 'Sterling', but otherwise unmarked, the cartouche has an inscription dated 1896. £150–£200.

183 American cigar stand with lighter, c. 1870. Regrettably unmarked, it would sell for £200–£300. A fully-marked example would retail for at least double this price.

184 Selection of pocket vesta cases, *top to bottom, left to right:* C.S.and F.S., Chester, 1912, £30-£40; American, *c.* 1900, £100-£120; F.D., Birmingham, 1906, £20-£30; A.and J. Zachery, Birmingham, 1900, £300-£400; H.and A., Chester, 1876, £300-£400.

sharp, metallic sound, whereas the plastic imitation sounds dull and heavy.

In the late Victorian and Edwardian periods vesta cases were made in many novelty shapes, including hearts, books, hats, shoes, animals and watches. There was even a macabre miniature coffin, a tiny cross in red enamel on its hinged lid; and a replica of an outside earth closet, the door opening to reveal a seated figure wearing a top hat! Most of these novelties were made in plate, although silver vesta cases were also combined with whistles, and stamp and sovereign cases.

Match and vesta boxes designed for table use also had silver sleeve covers, often standing on little ball feet. Recently Christie's South Kensington sold a set of four boxes engraved: 'Library, Dining-room, Sitting-room, and Study'. In the 1920s and 1930s, silver covers were even made for book matches. These seem to be little collected today. They were made for pocket use, replacing the vesta case described above, and are mostly engraved with initials, which possibly accounts for their apparent unpopularity. Matches were also kept in heavy spherical glass and pottery holders with plain silver mounts, the bowls ribbed with striations for striking each match. They are normally three to four inches in diameter, but occasionally one may come across a much larger example

In the last quarter of the nineteenth century, pocket lighters began to be used, their hollow bodies filled with fuel absorbed by a cotton wick, ignited by means of a sparking flint mechanism. Most early examples were of brass, but occasionally silver was used, and once again the Victorians found an ideal surface for enamelled decoration. In the

185 Wonderfully whimsical table vesta box formed as a parcel-gilt chimpanzee, with toffee-coloured glass eyes. E.C.B., London, 1867, £800-£1,000.

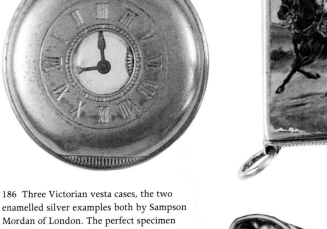

186 Three Victorian vesta cases, the two
enamelled silver examples both by Sampson
Mordan of London. The perfect specimen
made in 1879, £400-£500; the badly damaged
specimen made in 1897, £250-£350; the
novelty vesta case, c. 1890, modelled as a
pocket watch is made of electro-plated brass
with a plastic dial, £50-£70.

187 Many small pieces of silver were
decorated with a facsimile of the cover of
Punch magazine, either in enamelling,
engraving or stamping. This ashtray, made by
D.and F., Birmingham, 1899, would now cost
£100-£120.

188 Three novelty vesta cases, *left to right:*
C. and B., London, 1892, £250-£300; German
low-grade silver *c.* 1900, £200-£300;
American, stamped in the aesthetic style
popular *c.* 1870, £100-£120.

1920s and 1930s engine-turned Art Deco lighters were popular, some even inset with a tiny watch. These are now very saleable, particularly if made or retailed by Dunhills or Cartier. Many are still in working order, but damaged specimens can often be repaired with a relatively small outlay, so all will find a willing buyer.

Late Victorian and Edwardian table lighters are quite common. They were often made in the shape of a Roman lamp with serpent handle, or more amusingly, as a spherical bomb or grenade closely resembling those carried by the villain in a childrens' comic. This latter type was invariably weighted at the bottom, to ensure stability. Both should have a tiny wick-holder to transfer the flame to one's cigar, this often with a spiral-fluted handle or one decorated with a flame effect.

Table lighters were also made from silver-mounted antelope horns taken from hunting trophies, with the spiralling horns of the Indian Blackbuck being amongst the most popular. Such pieces are today perhaps the most acceptable of the many examples of the hunters 'art', produced in enormous quantities at the turn of the century by firms such as Rowland Ward of Piccadilly, who also made match holders and ashtrays from the hooves of favourite steeds. The most common design, patented by Elkington and Company of Birmingham, was in the shape of a fearsome dragon with one talon raised upon a ball, the flame issuing from the creature's gaping jaws. Some table lighters with antler or horn handles were set in two swivelling gimbels, rather like ships' lamps, so that they could be passed around the table, with no danger from spilt fuel. The lighters themselves were weighted so that they remained upright at all times, and some examples were even mounted on ivory wheels, to facilitate sliding along the table without scratching its polished surface. These are again mainly of late Victorian and Edwardian manufacture.

8 Personal Possessions

Scent Bottles and Vinaigrettes

Scent has long been used by both women and men, often in an attempt to mask unpleasant odours in an age when regular bathing was considered unnecessary, if not injurious to one's health! At the same time it was commonly believed that strong perfumes were a protection against pestilence. The wealthy carried boxes with sponges soaked in vinegar scented with lavender flowers and herbs and spices such as nutmeg, cinnamon, mint, and garlic. Rooms were sprinkled with perfumed powders or with rose and lavender water, and pastilles of concentrated perfume were also burnt.

Early silver scent bottles were usually flask-shaped, with finely-wrought chains so that they could be suspended from a chatelaine. Contemporary pouncet boxes and pomanders for spiced vinegar may also be found, although few specimens are marked. All are now rare and very expensive.

Fortunately there are still numerous examples of scent bottles from the eighteenth and nineteenth centuries. These were inexpensive trifles when first made, one firm selling the first quality 'flint-glass moulded perfume bottles' at two shillings per pound weight, this working out at about three farthings for each bottle. In the 1870s the Rotherham Glass Works listed 'smelling bottles various' at seven shillings a gross, selling them to the silver trade who made their little silver caps. Although rather neglected at one time, prices have risen considerably over the last few years. Georgian cut-glass specimens with tiny bright-cut silver screw or hinged tops and delightful coloured glass bottles, often enlivened with fine gilding, can still be found quite easily. Originally sold in protective leather or shagreen cases lined in plush, the presence of such a case can add fifty percent to the asking price.

This period also saw the introduction of the vinaigrette, a small box with tightly-fitting hinged lid. These were usually decorated with bright-cut engraving or engine-turning and had gilt linings to protect the silver from the acidic vinegar. Each contained a pierced grill concealing a sponge which was soaked with aromatic liquid. Carried by both men and women, the vinaigrette was seen as an essential fashion acces-

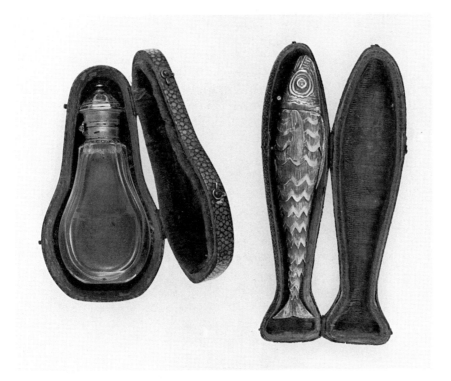

189 Two late seventeenth- or early eighteenth-century scent bottles, each in original plush-lined shagreen case. Both are unmarked, but were almost certainly made in Britain. £400-£500 each.

sory at the turn of the century. If one felt faint, a common sensation in the days of filthy and oppressive streets and over-tight corsets for both sexes, then a quick sniff at the pungent vinegar would clear the head, restoring the sickly back to vigorous health. In fact, one can still smell the scented vinegar in some examples, their sponges with faint, pleasant aromas lingering after many years of disuse.

While the majority of vinaigrettes were oblong, numerous novelty examples were introduced in the first quarter of the nineteenth century. One can find specimens shaped as purses, handbags, watches, books, lockets, articulated fish, flowers, crowns, and even skulls. Others were inset with polished agates or gemstones, the latter sometimes spelling out a word such as 'dearest' or 'regards' with the initial letters of their names. A third, more exotic, variety might be concealed within a fob-seal, or fitted with a tiny musical box movement. While such novelties are now very expensive, one can still find small oblong vinaigrettes for less than £100.

The vinaigrette was relatively short-lived. Although examples were still made in the Edwardian era, they were considered old-fashioned by the 1850s. At this time a new form of scent bottle was introduced, this consisting of a double-ended coloured glass cylinder, sometimes hinged in the centre, the two halves opening to reveal a locket or, more rarely, a vinaigrette. These double-ended bottles were designed to hold both perfume and aromatic vinegar or smelling salts, one end often fitted with a screw cap, the other with a hinged cap. Although cut clear glass examples with silver-gilt mounts were popular, the majority were made in brightly-coloured glass with plain facets and unmarked silver tops. Better examples might be encased in silver cage-work studded with turquoise, coral or split pearl beads. Specimens made from cased glass can also still be found. Here the outer layer of coloured glass is cut to reveal a clear glass interior. Double-ended scent bottles sell well today, especially if still complete with original fitted leather case. Several firms produced a variation on the theme of the double bottle, which hinged in the centre to take the shape of a pair of opera glasses. Rimmel sold many such

190 This collection of silver-topped glass scent bottles contains several unmarked examples. They all date from the period 1860-1880, with the exception of the bottle top left, which was made c. 1820. Four of the pieces on the bottom row have tiny chains and finger rings. £50-£200.

191 Egg-shaped bottles are now very collectable, particularly as each is unique, the porcelain bodies hand-painted to simulate a variety of wild birds' eggs. While most had simple, round screw caps, one can also find chicken and owl heads, and crowns, as illustrated here. £100-£300.

examples, an article in an 1869 edition of the *Englishwoman's Domestic Magazine* praising their novelty. Vinaigrettes were also combined with horn-shaped scent bottles, usually made of silver-gilt and with chains and finger rings. Sampson Mordan was the most prolific manufacturer of these popular and charming novelties.

In the second half of the nineteenth century novelty scent bottles became available. Many had pottery or porcelain bodies formed as nuts or fruit, and I have even seen several examples of bottles shaped and decorated as miniature 'willow pattern' plates. A particularly delightful

192 Selection of nineteenth-century bottles, including a silver specimen in case by Sampson Mordan and Co., London, 1886, engraved with Kate-Greenaway-style children. The illustration also shows two double-ended scent bottles, c. 1880, and a delightful example made from a seashell, the lid also by Sampson Mordan, London, 1879. £100-£300.

variety had porcelain, ovoid bodies painted to simulate the eggs of wild birds. Made in two sizes, the majority of these were fitted with plain screw tops manufactured by Sampson Mordan and Company, although one may also find rarer examples, their caps modelled as the heads of newly-hatched chicks. Although these pieces are still readily available, they are very popular today.

During the last quarter of the nineteenth century, scent bottles were often entirely encased in silver with delightful engraved or chased decoration. Most were smothered with bright-cut flowers and leaves,

193 Three Birmingham-made vinaigrettes: *left:* Nathaniel Mills, 1846, £200-£250; *centre:* George Unite, 1859; *right:* Joseph Taylor, 1810; £150-£200 each. Although pieces by Mills usually command much higher prices, this unusual book-shaped example has been spoiled, as someone has tried to remove a name, scratching it out clumsily and then engraving a later date onto the cartouche.

but Mordan made many examples engraved with eighteenth-century style children, his designs based on the drawings of Kate Greenaway. Unfortunately, many are now damaged, their tiny hinges sprained or split with years of use. Others have broken glass interiors, this often difficult to spot unless one can see a crack in the glass which appears at the neck of the bottle.

It is worth pursuing the special containers made to hold the products of the Crown Perfumery company, manufactured at the turn of the century. Each case was hinged to hold a bottle of perfume which was simply replaced when empty. Die-stamped with arabesques and often

194 Three combination scent bottles and vinaigrettes, each made by Sampson Mordan and Co. in the 1880s, and a Crown Perfumery heart-shaped scent bottle case die-stamped with cherubs, London, 1902. The first items would now cost £400-£500 each, but one could still find the latter priced at £100-£150.

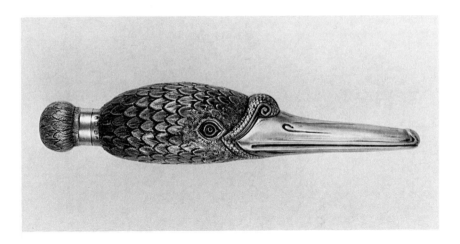

195 Rare swan's head bottle made in Birmingham, 1892. Almost seven inches long and very well made, with hand-chased feathers. £600-£800.

with an elaborate scroll cartouche, these delightful pieces were made in two shapes: a long tapering cylinder and a heart. Both types should still contain a Crown Perfumery bottle, preferably complete with paper label.

The twentieth century saw the introduction of mass-produced perfume sold in attractive moulded glass bottles which were pretty enough to carry in the handbag or to display on the dressing table. This signalled the beginning of the end of the scent bottle, and many must have been simply thrown away, as decanting became an unnecessary chore. In today's market however all are collected. 1920s and 1930s jars and bottles by Lalique can fetch a small fortune, and some people are even buying 1950s and 1960s examples produced by Avon and once sold from door to door, in the firm belief that such pieces will prove to be a good investment. It is hardly surprising that antique specimens are soaring in price, although the astute and patient buyer may still find charming Georgian and Victorian pieces without spending a fortune.

Visiting Card Cases

During the nineteenth and early twentieth centuries wealthy women, with their hosts of servants, had very little to do. Domestic duties were often limited to a brief consultation with cook or house-keeper in the morning, leaving the rest of the day for home crafts, letter writing, and good works. Paid employment was simply unthinkable, and even serious reading and study were considered unladylike. To relieve the tedium, a complicated system of visits was organized, and every week each family had an 'at home' day, when the ladies received callers. The visitors were expected to stay for only a few minutes, leaving to make room for the next group.

It became customary for each caller to carry cards, which were presented to the maid or butler, or left on a salver which stood on the hall table. Gradually this ceremony became more and more complicated, until society dictated that a married woman should leave one of her cards for each adult female in the family. She also had to leave two of her husband's cards. Some hostesses would display the cards of particularly honoured guests for weeks, until they became too dog-eared to be convincing. Conversely, one might receive unwelcome visitors. Their cards would be accepted, but the visitors themselves would be dismissed by the maid, who would bar the door with the chilling words: 'Not at home'. The sensitive knew that they had been rejected, but etiquette demanded that they leave without making a fuss. As Mrs Beeton explains: 'The form of words 'not at home' may be understood in different senses, but the only courteous way is to receive them as perfectly true'.

Card cases came in several distinct forms and sizes. Some had small lids with tiny hinges. Others had 'sleeve' lids which slid off completely. A third common type was modelled as a book with press button catch, releasing the two halves to reveal a kid-skin lining, often divided into compartments for cards and stamps. Many were also fitted with ivory *aide memoires* and tiny pencils. Harrods were still selling such pieces as late as 1929, their catalogue illustrating a 'Lady's silver card case' with pencil and *aide memoire*. This was priced at £2. 7s. 6d. if plain, an engine-turned case costing £2. 15s. 0d. Womens' card cases were larger than those used by men, presumably because they were carried in handbags rather than in tight breast pockets. Some of them may be five inches in length, while gentlemens' cases are often no longer than three and a half inches. They are also much slimmer and plainer, with no raised decoration to catch on pocket linings. Many examples were curved to fit waistcoat pockets, some with no lids, the cards simply sliding into a protective silver sleeve.

Victorian and Edwardian card cases are still readily available, although silver examples have now become expensive. The earliest ones date from the early 1800s and are simple in outline. By the 1830s shaped cases became popular. Many specimens were now of great quality, their

196 Four Birmingham-made visiting card cases, *left* to *right:* Walker and Hall, 1904, stamped with the ever-popular group of cherubs amidst clouds, £250-£300; A. and J. Zachery, 1902, stamped with an striking Art Nouveau maiden surrounded by arabesques, £300-£400; Nathaniel Mills, 1848. Castle-top cases are more expensive than their mass-produced counterparts, and this example depicts Windsor Castle, a tourist attraction still much visited today, £700-£900; C. and N., 1878, bright-cut and frosted in the aesthetic style influenced by Japanese art, £300-£350.

197 Combination card case and *aide memoire* complete with pencil, Nathaniel Mills, Birmingham, 1844. Made of red leather and with ivory leaves, the front and back covers are applied with silver plaques engine-turned and bright-cut with flowers. £400-£500.

heavy silver die-stamped with arabesques. Nathaniel Mills of Birmingham made some particularly fine examples at this time, decorated with cast and chased souvenir views of celebrated buildings. As the century progressed card cases became lighter. Most were decorated with bright-cut designs of flowers and foliage, each with a small cartouche for the initials of the owner. 'Aesthetic' cases with Japanese style decoration were popular in the 1870s and 1880s. Such designs incorporated frosting, parcel-gilding, and the obligatory engravings of birds and flowering branches within fan-shaped panels.

Machine-rolled silver examples made in the late nineteenth century were often of relatively poor quality. Nevertheless, they can look most impressive, the thin metal mounts stamped with elaborate arabesques, roses, or the popular group of cherubs peering from behind a bank of clouds. A more unusual specimen noted recently was stamped with *The Monarch of the Glen*, perhaps the most famous and widely-reproduced painting of the highly-popular Victorian artist, Landseer. Many card cases were fitted with fine chains and finger rings, presumably so that they could be carried during the evening. Edwardian and later card cases reverted to simplicity, although engine-turning became popular again, and novelty cases with revolving wheels pushing up one card at a time came into fashion.

While British card cases can still be found quite easily and cheaply, American examples are much rarer. Most seem to have been made by Albert Coles, a New York silversmith active in the second quarter of the nineteenth century. Usually engine-turned, his pieces are now much collected.

A Variety of Boxes

198 George III étui with several original fittings, including an ear pick and a bleeding knife. Joseph Taylor, Birmingham, 1801, £400-£600.

Étuis, or tapering oblong cases with hinged lids, are still quite common. They date from the early eighteenth century, although many examples are unmarked. Some were made entirely of silver, often finely-chased with delightful rococo decoration, while others were covered in shagreen, with reeded silver mounts. They were designed for several purposes: the most simple were intended to hold tiny glass scent bottles with screw tops. Larger étuis were fitted with a selection of handy accessories such as pencils, ivory *aide memoires*, snuff spoons, folding scissors, and even sets of miniscule cutlery with detachable tapering hollow handles. The travelling surgeon might well carry a similar box fitted with several razor-sharp bleeding knives, the steel blades of which folded into tortoiseshell or mother-of-pearl handles. These were used for the practice of phlebotomy, which involved cutting into a vein to release some blood. It was generally believed that this would alleviate a variety of maladies ranging from migraine headaches and gout to madness and 'frenzy'. Today it is rare to find an étui complete with all original fittings. Most have several gaps or are totally empty. One may be able to

199 Charles II counter box complete with a collection of gaming counters, the latter engraved with the *Cries of London*, unmarked, c. 1670. The engraving is of the finest quality, and the inside of the lid is stamped with a portrait of the monarch. £2,000-£3,000.

find contemporary accessories elsewhere, thus recreating a complete, if imperfect, set.

Small circular gaming boxes with lift-off covers were popular in the seventeenth and eighteenth centuries. Each originally contained a set of counters used for gambling, or for working out difficult sums. Made from either solid metal or filigree, the majority were unmarked, although the Birmingham craftsmen of the late eighteenth century sent many examples up for assay. Sometimes these were struck with a portrait of Queen Anne, misleading one to assume a much earlier date of manufacture. Seventeenth-century counter boxes are usually scratch-engraved with stylized leaves and flowers and their counters had similar crude decoration. Some finer examples have survived however, each counter engraved with a different scene, perhaps of a Biblical or classical subject, or from the *Cries of London* series illustrating city street vendors as they 'cried their wares'. Later specimens were usually bright-cut, some containing a collection of worn sixpenny pieces although others had purpose-made counters.

The late eighteenth century saw the introduction of a new type of counter box, its lid fitted with a revolving pointer and engraved with a frieze of numbers. This type was used entirely for gambling, along with Victorian silver-mounted wooden bezique and whist-markers and cribbage-scorers. A further sporting curiosity is the turn-of-the-century butt selector, a small silver box similar to a vesta case (see chapter 7) but fitted with six to ten numbered ivory pegs. Each guest would choose a peg at random, its number matching that of one of the shooting positions. Thus everyone could be satisfied that the host had shown no favouritism.

The earliest known patchbox bears hallmarks for 1669, although the curious practice of decorating the face with cut-out paper shapes or 'court plasters' was recorded some thirty years earlier. Traditionally first used by a woman to disguise her smallpox scars, the fashion swept across Europe until the most elegant of both sexes were speckled with false

200 George III counter box, Samuel Pemberton, Birmingham, 1799. This unusual piece has a revolving pointer, used for various games of chance. £200-£300. *Photograph by courtesy of the Birmingham Assay Office.*

beauty spots. Not content with round patches, the more extravagantly fashionable wore stars, crescent moons, diamonds, galleons, and other strange shapes. While seventeenth century patchboxes were raised from a sheet of flat silver, later examples were usually constructed from thin metal with applied rims. Most were circular or oval, until the mid eighteenth century when elliptical specimens became fashionable. All were originally inset with a mirror, glued inside the lift-off or hinged cover so that the patches could be placed with ease.

Eighteenth-century toothpick boxes can be confused with patchboxes, although most date from the 1780s, some twenty years after the demise of the patch as a fashion accessory. Once again their lids are inset with mirrors, and many are also lined with plush. Boat-shaped and oblong specimens are still quite common, many of them made by Samuel Pemberton, one of the most skilful Birmingham silversmiths. Too shallow and narrow to be confused with similarly-decorated snuff boxes, these delicate pieces now sell quite well. Cheaper toothpick boxes made

201 Although circular sovereign cases are still common, larger examples have become quite scarce. This example is unusual, as it contains spaces for sovereigns, half sovereigns, and stamps. R.C., Birmingham, 1900, £200-£250.

202 *Right:* unusual pocket butt selector, Birmingham, 1932. Although one of the ivory pegs is now lost, this could sell for £300-£400.

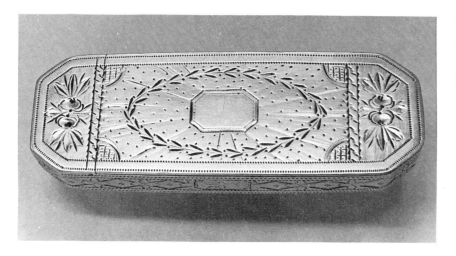

203 George III bright-cut tooth-pick box with concealed hinge, the lid inset with a tiny mirror, Samuel Pemberton, Birmingham, 1791. Although beautifully made, such pieces are still under priced. £120-£150. *Photograph by courtesy of the Birmingham Assay Office.*

from ivory can also still be found, their lids often applied with a minia-ture, or a panel of woven hair surrounded by an unmarked gold mount.

Throughout the late eighteenth and nineteenth centuries the daughters of the wealthy were encouraged to be 'artistic', to take singing or piano lessons or to indulge in fancy embroidery. Watercolour painting was considered a particularly ladylike accomplishment, and vast numbers of amateur pictures still survive. Watercolour boxes were pro-duced by several silversmiths, each with interior compartments for the blocks of colour and the brush, their hinged lid acting as the mixing palette. Most have a swivelling loop handle for the thumb, to enable the artist to hold the box securely and comfortably in one hand while paint-ing with the other. Georgian watercolour boxes are now quite rare and expensive.

204 Regency watercolour box larger and more sophisticated than most, with three depressions for mixing paints and a space for storage of brushes. Made by William Bateman, London, 1820, this example is six inches long. £600-£800.

205 Three Edwardian sovereign cases and two stamp cases, all made in Birmingham in the early 1900s. £40-£60 each.

Judging from the number which survive, one can assume that sovereign cases were extremely popular in the late Victorian and Edwardian periods. Most were designed to hang from gentlemen's watch chains and were therefore fitted with tiny suspension loops, although I have also seen desk top versions with apertures for several coins. The commonest type of circular sovereign case contained one or two sovereigns, held securely in place by a sprung disc. The more wealthy could buy oblong combination sovereign and half sovereign cases. Even triple examples exist, usually also oblong but more rarely triangular in shape. A case was also devised for both coins and stamps. Most were relatively plain, with simple engine-turned or bright-cut decoration. All are now collected as they now make unusual and attractive pieces of jewellery.

Posy Holders

Small bunches of sweet-smelling flowers and herbs were carried by our ancestors from medieval times to ward off the plague. Although ineffective, the floral perfumes at least made life pleasanter, in an age when streets were invariably foul-smelling and filthy, and personal hygiene was almost unknown.

By the nineteenth century sanitary conditions in fashionable and expensive parts of the city had improved considerably. Nevertheless,

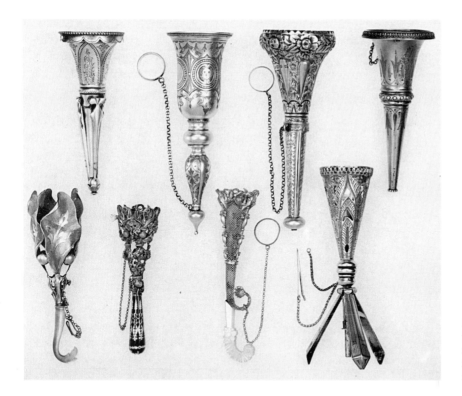

206 Group of Victorian posy holders, three of them hallmarked in 1873, 1842, and 1894, the rest unmarked. One example has tripod legs mounted on springs. When not in use, they fold back to form the handle. £150-£350 each.

flowers were still carried or worn by smart women, and many magazines gave detailed instructions on how to make small bouquets or posies. Obviously there was a danger that fine clothing might be spoiled by droplets of water, and so the silver posy holder was created, its handle enclosing the wet stems of the flowers. In America these objects were known as 'tussie mussies', the first part of this name originating in an old English word for a nosegay. The second part may well refer to the wet moss used to keep the flowers fresh, although by Victorian times many posy holders were packed with cotton wadding soaked in strong scent, thus enhancing the natural fragrance of the flowers.

Although the posy holder was basically a small container, usually with a carrying handle, several types soon developed. The most common were the cornet and the cornucopia, but other examples were formed as flowers or baluster-shaped vases. Because it was difficult to put down a posy holder without crushing the floral arrangement, many were fitted with three sprung legs, which folded back to form the handle. This tripod type was particularly useful for wedding bouquets. Many specimens were also fitted with chains and finger rings, enabling a lady to dance with ease, her posy swinging from her hand. While most examples secured the flowers by means of a long pin, more elaborate posy holders had sprung clamps or hinged 'petals' which opened and closed according to the adjustment of a moveable ring.

Many nineteenth-century posy holders were made entirely of silver, often stamped with flowers, leaves, and vines or applied with fili-gree Gothic decoration. Very few examples were marked, doubtless

207 Unmarked filigree horn-shaped posy holder with finger ring and brooch mount, c. 1875, £150-£200.

because their fragile nature might not withstand the rigours of testing and hallmarking. Large numbers of posy holders were made using combinations of various materials. Specimens might be applied with beads of turquoise, coral, or paste, or decorated with seed pearls. Others had plaques of painted porcelain or enamel, or were fitted with tiny mirrors so that a lady could see who was in the room without turning her head. Many examples had turned ivory or mother-of-pearl handles, and innumerable inexpensive posy holders were made of silver-plated or gilt brass, these cheap pieces often given away as souvenirs at balls.

While most posy holders were between four and six inches in height, smaller versions were manufactured for little girls to carry. Tiny specimens were also made for gentlemen's buttonholes or to be worn as jewellery. These small examples are much cheaper than their larger equivalents.

Further Dress Accessories

There remains a wide range of silver dress articles yet to be explored, with numerous examples surviving, particularly from the mid nineteenth century. Even Georgian pieces are still available in large numbers, and can be bought by the modest collector.

Buckles were highly prized in the eighteenth century, when fashion dictated that they be worn on shoes, breeches, sashes, belts, cravats, and even hats. It is estimated that two and a half million various buckles

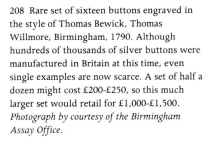

208 Rare set of sixteen buttons engraved in the style of Thomas Bewick, Thomas Willmore, Birmingham, 1790. Although hundreds of thousands of silver buttons were manufactured in Britain at this time, even single examples are now scarce. A set of half a dozen might cost £200-£250, so this much larger set would retail for £1,000-£1,500. *Photograph by courtesy of the Birmingham Assay Office.*

209 Single turn-of-the-century buttons are becoming increasingly difficult to find, as so many have been converted into spurious pieces of jewellery. £5-£8 each, although cased sets of six will retail for at least £100.

were manufactured in Birmingham each year, although, sadly, few remain in good condition. Silver was too soft for everyday use, so the majority had steel pins and fittings with thin silver mounts, often decorated with faceting so that the buckles sparkled as if set with precious stones. Because these mounts became worn and the steel fittings fell prey to rust, perfect Georgian buckles are now rare. Nevertheless, they are not expensive as they cannot be used today. Victorian and Edwardian belt buckles are far more collected, particularly as it is still traditional in Great Britain for a nursing sister to wear a silver buckle as part of her uniform. This constant demand has ensured a continuous rise in price.

Many late nineteenth-century buckles are highly ornate, with cast and pierced arabesque decoration. Others were influenced by Art Nouveau fashions, incorporating delicate sprays of flowers and maidens with flowing hair. All are now reproduced from casts of originals. One must therefore always check the hallmarks with great care, as appearances may be deceptive. American buckles were often more innovative than British examples, each manufacturer creating new designs to capture the imagination of the market. According to *Jewelers' Circular*, a late nineteenth-century trade magazine, there were buckles designed for the 'bicycle and athletic girl, yachting, skating, golf, horses, military, dancing, and old-fashioned girl', a list which must surely have covered almost every taste.

Turn-of-the-century belts are generally less saleable than buckles, as they are simply too small for most women to wear today. Made at a time when the tiny 'wasp waist' was fashionable, some measure no more than eighteen inches in length. Many are now broken up, their links converted into brooches and the buckles sold off separately.

The chatelaine, an arrangement of chains and clips fastened to a brooch mount or, more commonly, to a belt hook, was known in Roman

210 Selection of late Victorian belt buckles, all made in Birmingham. £100-£200.

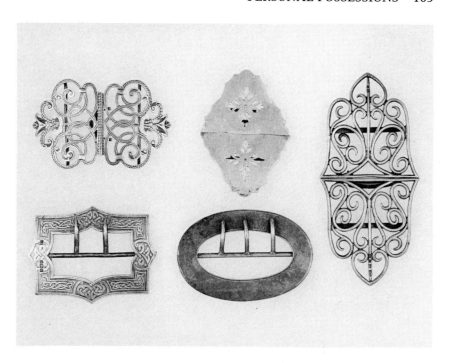

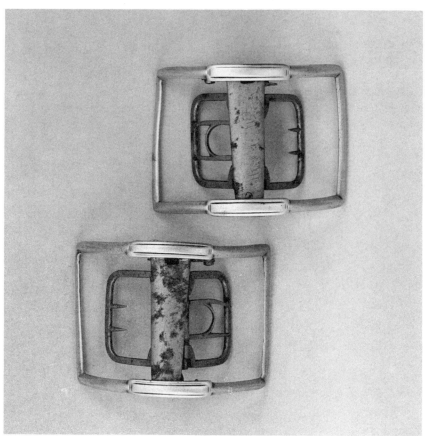

211 Georgian silver-mounted steel shoe buckles are still inexpensive, if of British manufacture. American examples are quite rare however, costing £600-£800 per pair, if in good condition. These, by Myer Myers, New York, c. 1780, are identical to British buckles of the same period.

times, and survived almost unchanged until large pockets were introduced for women, in the late 1800s. They were worn by housewives or housekeepers, the numerous chains carrying a wide range of useful objects such as keys, note pads, pencils, vesta cases, and sewing equipment. Early examples were often simple and functional, but later both the chatelaines themselves and their fittings became increasingly ornate, with elaborate stamped and pierced mounts. Decoration was often based loosely on eighteenth-century rococo designs, although some examples were influenced by prevailing Art Nouveau taste. Vast numbers were

212 Three Victorian chatelaines, two with belt clips, the third complete with a matching panelled belt. *Left* to *right:* William Comyns, London, 1898, with two *aide memoires,* a pencil, and an expanding mesh purse, £250-£300; D.and F., Birmingham, 1892, with a vesta case and a pair of folding scissors, £600-£800; the Sterling Company, Providence, Rhode Island, *c.* 1890, with a collection of steel keys and a pair of scissors, £250-£300.

213 Four purses made in Chester in the late nineteenth century, each lined in leather and with a chain and finger ring. Manufactured from thin sheet silver. £60-£80 each.

214 Continental handbag mount with belt clip, £150-£200, and an *aide memoire* with ivory leaves, £60-£80, both imported by Berthold Muller, with import marks for Chester 1898, and London 1879.

made, both in Britain and America, and the late nineteenth-century silversmiths experimented with many new designs. American manufacturers were particularly adventurous, introducing novelty ideas such as serpents, birds, ships' wheels, and yachts. Chatelaines are now avidly collected, particularly if still complete with the original fittings.

Sewing equipment is also popular today, and there are a great many collectors of needle cases, scissors, tape measures, pin wheels, and the like. 'Sewing eggs' or 'acorns' are especially charming. Their lids unscrew to reveal a tiny spool for cotton nestling inside a thimble. Thimbles have a particularly large following. Early specimens can be recognized by their irregular hand-punching, while Georgian examples are often decorated with applied filigree work or gemstones. Many souvenir thimbles, stamped with views of famous landmarks or with pious verses, were produced during the nineteenth century, as were advertising pieces. Sadly, many were not hallmarked or have become worn through use, leaving the collector to guess at both age and origin. While British thimbles were originally exported to America, colonial silversmiths soon began to manufacture them. An example by Paul Revere can be seen in the Boston Museum of Art, and, by 1790, Benjamin Halstead had opened a 'Thimble Manufactury' in New York City. The nineteenth century saw the establishment of several new firms specializing in making thimbles, while larger companies also recognized their money-making potential. In the 1830s, Gorham, Webster and Price set up a small workshop devoted to silver thimbles at the back of their factory in Providence. Many American examples are elaborate, with engraved floral borders or stamped arabesque decoration. As in Britain, souvenir thimbles were also popular, and special pieces were produced to commemorate occasions such as the World's Fair of 1853. American thimbles are collected as keenly as their British counterparts.

215 Seven turn-of-the-century silver thimbles including two stamped with advertisements, a souvenir example stamped: 'Leeds', and a gilt example decorated with enamelling. £10-£50.

As one searches through the trays of small items in antique shops, one may come across some rather puzzling clips, often hand-shaped and usually attached to a long chain with finger ring. These useful gadgets were clipped onto skirt and petticoats which could then be raised slightly to avoid the dust. Today these curiosities often go unrecognized and, as a result, may sell for very little.

Buttons became widely popular in the eighteenth century, and thousands of workers were soon involved in their manufacture, producing examples in many different materials, shapes, and sizes. Servants' liveries were embellished with several rows of buttons, each normally engraved with a crest. While some of these can be identified, many are totally spurious, *nouveau riche* families simply designing their own crests to keep up with their aristocratic neighbours. Special silver buttons were also made for regiments, hunts, and societies, while delightful paste-set specimens were used to add sparkle. Many silversmiths specialized in these small objects, both here and in America, and the Birmingham silversmiths produced sets of charming buttons finely-engraved with animals and hunting scenes, their designs often copied from the wood engravings of the Newcastle artist Thomas Bewick. Regrettably, plain Georgian buttons have often been 'enhanced' with later decoration. This is usually too crude to confuse the astute buyer, who may even be able to detect the traces of an erased crest beneath the modern engraving.

In the nineteenth century buttons were often heavily cast and chased, with patterns closely following those of contemporary buckles

216 Victorian skirt-lifter, made in Birmingham 1876, £10-£20.

and chatelaines. Often sold in fitted leather cases, they are still quite common unlike their earlier counterparts, and turn-of-the-century buttons may be found for less than £5 each.

Silver was also used in the manufacture of handbags, purses, and wallets, often in conjunction with needlework, leather, and crocodile skin. Georgian handbag mounts were usually decorated with cut facets. Silver-mounted seashell purses were also popular in the early nineteenth century, often lined with brightly-coloured moire silk. Victorian handbags were far larger than their earlier counterparts. Ornate embossed mounts were sold by craft shops, the customer embroidering her own bag from one of the many Berlin woolwork patterns available throughout the nineteenth century. Large numbers of small bags were produced in the late nineteenth century, mainly by the small-workers of Birmingham and Chester. These had thinly-rolled silver mounts, frequently engine-turned or stamped to simulate crocodile skin. Flimsy and easily damaged, they were soon replaced by mesh bags and purses with plain mounts, often made abroad and therefore with import hallmarks. Many are impressively Art Deco, with graduated fringes or ball and drop tassels. These too were fragile. Nevertheless they sell well, doubtless because of the current craze for 1930s styles.

Finally, silver-handled malacca walking sticks and parasols were produced in large numbers throughout the last century, many with simple mushroom-shaped knobs decorated with flowers and engraved

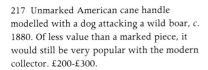

217 Unmarked American cane handle modelled with a dog attacking a wild boar, c. 1880. Of less value than a marked piece, it would still be very popular with the modern collector. £200-£300.

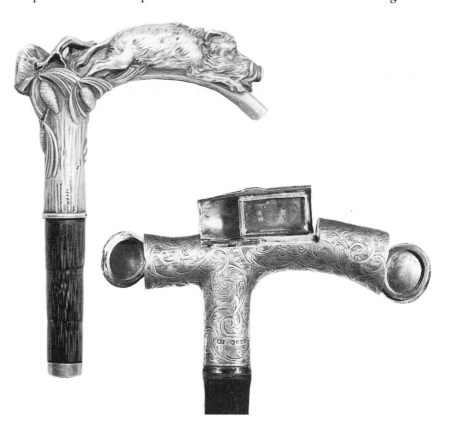

218 *Right:* this unusual cane handle contains a sovereign case, a vesta case, a snuff box and a cheroot holder. Made by Ebenezer Newman, London, 1887, it appeals both to collectors of silver novelties and walking sticks. £600-£800.

with initials. Others had stags' horn handles with silver ring mounts, and some were more elaborate still, their curved crook handles mounted entirely in 'fluted, rope, repousse, scroll, flower and heraldic' silver, according to a late nineteenth century advertisement for the J.F. Fradley Company of New York. At much the same time Tiffany and Co. were producing fine examples 'of hammered silver with enrichments of colored alloys and other metals, $15 to $45', while their umbrellas were claimed to be 'of superior English silk, woven for the purpose, and more pliable and closer than the ordinary weighted or prepared silks, which are liable to cut'. Both walking sticks and parasols are keenly collected today, particularly if made by a celebrated manufacturer. Novelty specimens sell well, even if unmarked, and the collector should be on the look out for sticks which contain match boxes, watches, compasses, tubes for cigars, corkscrews, and spirit flasks.

219 While silver belts are still quite common, silver and tortoiseshell examples have become difficult to find. Sadly, few women can wear them today, as they were made in an era when corsets guaranteed a wasp waist, usually of no more than 18 inches. William Comyns, London, 1892, £600-£800.

9 Silver for Children

Mugs and Beakers

Silver has been used for many centuries in the manufacture of christening presents, the most traditional gift being a spoon. Affluent god-parents might give a complete set of thirteen spoons, with the cast finials depicting Christ and his twelve apostles, while children in more humble circumstances would be satisfied with a single spoon, often made of pewter.

The majority of christening presents were, of course, inscribed with the initials of the recipient, and the date of his or her birth, some even recording the time of arrival and the weight of the baby. It is also quite common to find the names of the proud god-parents. One seventeenth century spoon recorded in Eric Delieb's *Investing in Silver*, 1970, was engraved with the charming verse:

> 'Rich. Elnor. Joane
> At Ye Font Stone
> Their word did give
> How you shouldst live',

a reference to the vows taken by the god-parents during the christening ceremony. Many nineteenth-century pieces were engraved with moral verses, exhorting the child to be noble, virtuous, and wise.

Mugs or tankards with handles, and beakers without, were often given as christening presents, although they were also traditionally used for serving hot drinks, as it was commonly believed that pottery vessels could affect the flavour. A broadsheet written in 1672 claimed: 'the smell and taste of Mock China bowls' would taint a hot beverage, spoiling its delicate aroma and taste. The widespread use of silver for this purpose means that one cannot state categorically whether a specific piece was designed for use by a child or an adult, although a contemporary presentation inscription may give some clues about the age of the original owner. Certainly, many examples were used by children, and some schools even listed mugs amongst the requisite items a boy should take with him to boarding school, as is mentioned in an advertisement in a 1789 issue of the *Birmingham Gazette*.

Early mugs are now very expensive. Attractively plain and sturdy, they fall outside the price range which most collectors can afford. Georgian mugs are comparatively common however, and good examples can still be found quite easily. Most are of a plain baluster shape, raised up from a sheet of silver by hammering the metal over a wooden stake. An applied rim was often added to give extra strength. Up to the third quarter of the eighteenth century, the majority were hallmarked underneath the base, where the punches were stamped in a haphazard circle. Later Georgian mugs were generally marked in a line just below the rim, usually to the right of the scroll handle.

The barrel-shaped mug first appeared in the 1760s, and remained in fashion for the next century or so. It was made from a tube of rolled sheet metal joined with a soldered seam often concealed by the handle. The barrel shape was often enhanced with engraved hoops and staves, or with chased body bands of reeding. Some similarly decorated mugs were manufactured with flaring bodies. These were especially popular in the Regency period.

By the mid nineteenth century mugs had become far more ornate in form and decoration. The thistle, or campana shape became popular. Here the vessel was raised on a chased pedestal foot and often with applied or chased floral and foliate decoration. Other mugs were enhanced with Gothic-style arches, their panels bright-cut with flowers and fruit, or with charming scenes of children at play. Ornate Victorian christening mugs are now very much collected, and fine examples in good condition can sell for as much as their plainer Georgian counterparts. Many of the best were made by the Barnard family of silversmiths from heavy, thick metal. One can still find lighter specimens with pretty engraved decoration. Many of these date from the 1870s and 1880s.

Twentieth-century silversmiths manufactured christening mugs in large quantities, generally reproducing earlier styles. Of the twelve

220 Two American mid-eighteenth-century mugs made in Boston, each identical to contemporary British mugs although very much rarer. *Left:* Samuel Minott; *right:* Joseph Loring. These sturdy and simple pieces are in great demand, retailing for £1,500-£2,000. An English equivalent might cost £700-£1,000.

221 Tumbler cup and three mugs: *left* to *right:* James Stamp, London, 1779, £500-£600; I.H., London, 1787, £400-£500; T.R., London, 1680, £700-£900; Charles Farley, Portland, Maine, *c.* 1815, £800-£1,000.

222 Selection of nineteenth-century christening mugs, all London made. *Left* to *right:* William Bateman, 1827, here the baluster shape of the eighteenth century has been enhanced with fine rococo chasing, £300-£400; C.E., 1894, a typical Victorian reproduction in the Carolean style, £200-£250; T.S., 1872, this simple mug has bright-cut floral swag decoration. It is made from extremely thin metal however, and is therefore less popular than the others, £100-£120; Messrs. Barnard, 1859, a heavy piece with cast handle, again enhanced with bright-cutting, £500-£600; William Hutton and Sons Ltd., 1900, heavy but rather dull, the presence of an inscription would deter most buyers, £150-£200.

designs illustrated in the Army and Navy Stores 1935-1936 catalogue, only two are modern. All the others are copies or adaptations, including a 'Charles II pattern Heavy Silver' example priced at £6. Art Nouveau mugs dating from the beginning of the century are quite rare, and the collector seeking a specimen in a typically twentieth-century style would have more chance of finding an Art Deco piece. Mugs made in this century are still available in large numbers, and one should still be able to find an attractive example very easily.

Many beakers were small, plain pieces, designed for the traveller. Some had leather cases, and were fitted with folding cutlery and tiny

223 Three American nineteenth-century mugs: *left* to *right:* T.and W., *c.* 1850, this maker has not yet been traced, resulting in a low value, £200-£300; L. and W., retailed by Stebbins and Co., New York, *c.* 1840, a known American retailer makes this piece more interesting to the collector, £300-£400; H.Harding and Co., Boston, *c.* 1830, although crude in manufacture, this mug is well marked, hence a higher price, £600-£800.

condiments to form a complete canteen for those who distrusted the vessels available in inns, or who were on military service. Others had heavy, rounded bases, so that they would maintain their balance during a journey in a rattling coach. These 'tumbler cups', often made by provincial silversmiths, were popular in both Britain and America throughout the seventeenth and eighteenth centuries, and the diarist Samuel Pepys records the purchase of a pair in 1664. Today they can be expensive, although eighteenth-century specimens are usually lighter in gauge and therefore less popular.

Taller, flat-bottomed beakers from the seventeenth and eighteenth centuries are uncommon, although bright-cut examples made in the 1780s and 1790s can still be found, many of them produced by the Bateman family of London. Victorian beakers are far more common, although few were made as christening presents. Most were designed as presentation cups, their inscriptions recording events as diverse as agricultural shows, sporting fixtures, and military shooting matches. These large pieces are relatively unsaleable. Novelty collapsable beakers, often fitting into a small circular box when not in use, and smaller beakers designed for children are more desirable. Although the collapsable beakers were primarily designed for picnic use, two plated examples are included under the heading 'Children's Cups' in the Montgomery Ward catalogue.

224 Unusual Victorian collapsible beaker, Edward Hutton, London, 1875, £200-£300.

Bowls and Porringers

Bowls and porringers were often given to young children, although many seventeenth- and eighteenth-century examples are quite large, indicating that use was not limited to infants. Confusingly, the British shallow vessel with one handle is usually called a 'cupping' or 'bleeding' bowl, the name referring to their frequent use in the common medical practise of bleeding a patient. This type of vessel is always called a porringer in America. In Britain the term 'porringer' describes a two-handled deeper vessel, known across the Atlantic as a caudle cup. For the sake of

225 Three American eighteenth-century bowls of the type commonly given as christening presents, each engraved with the initials of the original owner. *Left* to *right:* Samuel Casey, Exeter and South Kingston, Rhode Island, *c.* 1750; Samuel Minott, Boston, *c.* 1760; attributed to Samuel Vernon, Newport, *c.* 1715, but overstruck with the mark of John Tanner, Newport, £1,000-£1,500 each.

clarity, I will describe the type of vessel with one handle as a 'porringer' throughout this chapter, and refer to the other by the more general term 'bowl'.

In the late seventeenth century tall bowls came into popular use in Britain. These were often chased with fluting and moulded body bands, a decoration which served to strengthen the thin silver sides. Many also had large cartouches surrounded by scrolls and scalework, and crudely-stamped friezes of stylized flowers and acorns around their rims. Better examples had cast caryatid handles soldered onto their bowls, while more simple specimens were applied with wirework scroll handles. The majority of these 'Queen Anne' bowls are light and flimsy, and the collector must be careful to inspect for splits or patches.

In America the hammered porringer remained popular well into the eighteenth century. The earliest specimens had flat-bottomed circular bowls with straight sides, applied with a single cast handle decorated with piercing. By the 1720s most had bowls with domed centres and bellied sides. Unmarked specimens can often be identified by the patterns in their pierced handles, as each centre of the silver trade used a slightly different design. Perhaps the most common today is the 'key-hole' variety, distinguished by a keyhole-shaped aperture at the end of the handle. Although American eighteenth-century porringers are not rare, they are highly collectable, and good, marked examples may sell for many hundreds if not thousands of pounds, depending on age and town of manufacture. While the porringer maintained its popularity in America throughout the eighteenth century, in Great Britain a more graceful vase-shaped bowl replaced the 'Queen Anne' type in the 1760s. These pieces, often without handles, and usually decorated with bright-cut neo-classical engraving, are now quite rare.

The nineteenth century saw the introduction of a heavier, sqatter style, often chased with a broad frieze of rising flutes and with applied gadroon or chevron rims. This style is less attractive and consequently less expensive than its elegant George III predecessor. In the Victorian

226 Three British christening bowls copying the styles of the seventeenth and early eighteenth centuries. Such reproduction pieces were very popular at the turn of the century. The latter two examples are of excellent quality, each made in the higher Britannia Standard used during the reign of Queen Anne. *Left* to *right:* P.H., London, 1883, £80–£120; Goldsmiths and Silversmiths Co. Ltd., London, 1925, £250–£300; George Fox, London, 1905, £300–£400.

era, christening bowls were more obviously designed for children. Floral and foliate chasing became commonplace, and some examples were decorated with charming vignettes of children at play. Sampson Mordan and Co. produced some particularly pleasing pieces. At the turn of the century most silversmiths produced pieces in traditional 'antique' styles, suggesting earlier designs with spot-hammering, and cut-card and strap-work decoration. These reproductions are often surprisingly heavy and are of excellent quality. However, they are relatively unpopular today.

Although few examples of christening bowls were made during the Art Nouveau period in Britain, American makers exploited the style, producing lovely pieces with hand-hammered undulating surfaces decorated with naturalistic ornamentation. These are now highly collected, especially if by well-known firms such as Tiffany or Gorham. Gorham made some particularly wonderful pieces decorated with hammering and with exquisite flowing forms. This 'martelé' silver, (the name derives from the French word for hammered), was introduced to Gorham's range in the late 1800s. New pieces were developed for the 1900 Paris Exposition, and proved to be extremely popular. Nevertheless, the output remained quite small, as each piece required a tremendous amount of work for its creation. Martelé silver is now very expensive, particularly in America.

227 Late Victorian christening bowl in a fitted case, with a spoon and a napkin ring, Martin Hall and Co., Sheffield, 1898. Sets in fitted cases sell for about thirty percent more than loose examples, as they make ideal gifts today. £300–£400.

Rattles and Teething-Sticks

Silver-mounted rattles and teething-sticks have been traditional christening presents for many years. They were often referred to in Elizabethan inventories, and, in 1519, William Horman wrote: 'I wyll bye a rattell to styll my baby for cryenge'. Many portraits of children also show rattles and teething-sticks, often hung on a gaily-coloured ribbon and suspended around the child's neck.

Most rattles had coral handles, often scratched with tiny teeth marks from generations of teething babies. Indeed, some specimens have handles chewed down to a small stump, an obvious testimony to their effectiveness. Coral was smooth and cool, helping to alleviate the ache of tender gums. It was also used, more importantly, to guard the infant against the malevolent threat of witchcraft, a very real fear in the minds of our ancestors. Coral enjoyed an ancient reputation as a protection

228 Selection of nineteenth-century whistle rattles, all made in Birmingham. Each has a coral handle, although the example in the centre has been worn down to a stump by several generations of teething babies. Most had several bells to amuse the child, although whistles without this refinement are not unusual. £300-£500.

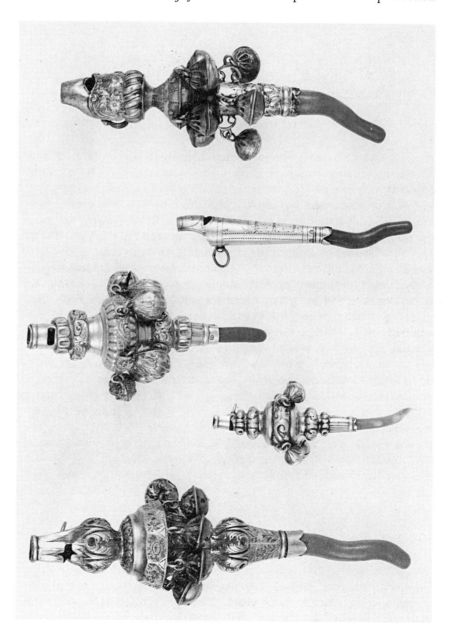

229 Edwardian reproduction rattle, made by C.C., Chester, 1905, £200-£250.

230 Two novelty rattles with hollow bodies filled with dried peas, each with a mother-of-pearl teething handle. *Left:* Humpty Dumpty, D.and N., Chester, 1922, £120-£150; *right:* a Kate Greenaway-style girl, C.S.and F.S., Birmingham, 1931, £120-£150.

from the Evil Eye, and the Romans festooned their babies' cradles with small pieces threaded onto strings. Although this practice died away, the belief in the benign influence of coral persisted for centuries, and the material was commonly used both for rattle handles and for jewellery.

Most early rattles had small bells attached, and many also had a whistle mouth-piece, the two combining to create a noisy toy which might amuse a restless child for hours on end. Generally made from thin silver, rattles can vary enormously in size and decoration, although the basic baluster shape changed little until the late nineteenth century. Georgian examples are usually quite small and delicate, with bright-cut floral and foliate swags and sprays. Later specimens are often much larger, their size allowing the introduction of heavy chased decoration.

Late nineteenth- and twentieth-century rattles rarely have coral handles. By now, mother-of-pearl, ivory, and even plastic were used, and most examples have a teething-ring handle rather than a stick handle. The bells also began to disappear at this time, and instead most rattles had a hollow body filled with loose, dried peas, providing enough noise to pacify the most restless baby. While later rattles are often less attractive than the earlier ones, there are several novelty types which are collected today. Figural rattles with bodies stamped out in the shape of teddy bears, policemen, Mr Punch, or the man in the moon, are all now popular. Another amusing type of rattle is stamped with two babies' faces, one crying and distorted with rage, the other smiling contentedly as if calmed by the rattle itself. Occasionally one may find a silver-gilt or silver-mounted stick of coral without bells or whistle, designed to act as a pacifier or teething-stick for a young baby. Examples in good condition are rare and quite expensive.

While early rattles and teething-sticks were often unmarked, eighteenth-century and later specimens should bear a full set of hallmarks. These can normally be found on the scalloped handle mount, although the maker's initials are usually stamped onto the whistle terminal. In many cases, the marks on the handle mount are partially obliterated with solder, due to careless replacement of lost or broken corals. Twentieth-century rattles were generally marked on the main body of the silver, and one will often find that the punches are divided, with some stamped onto each half of the hollow body. Rattles were manufactured and assayed throughout Britain, with examples from Birmingham being the most common. These were produced in large numbers from the 1770s, their manufacture continuing to the present day.

Christening Sets

Although spoons have long been a traditional gift for the new-born child, the christening set in fitted case made its appearance only at the very end of the eighteenth century. Most early sets consisted of two or three pieces, the various items sometimes made by different silversmiths. This is because each maker was a specialist, some manufacturing flatware and others hollow-ware such as knife handles. Existing patterns were often adapted for christening sets, but some new designs were also created, particularly after the widespread adoption of die-stamping in both Sheffield and Birmingham. Sets with hollow tubular handles stamped with shells and scrolls became popular; these were usually of poor quality and often gilded to create a misleadingly splendid effect.

By the mid nineteenth century christening sets were usually of better quality, the thicker gauge of silver combining with the protection afforded by their fitted cases, to ensure that the modern collector has a large number from which he may choose. Most will be engraved with the

231 American Art Nouveau mixed metal christening set decorated with spot-hammering, the bowl and the napkin ring applied with copper and brass fish and water-weeds. Regrettably, the pieces are not marked. £600-£800.

232 Standard Edwardian set in case, each piece bright-cut with arabesques and engraved with a monogram, Hilliard and Thomason, Birmingham, 1903, £80-£120. They are more popular if without initials, selling for £150-£200.

233 This attractive christening bowl and stand, decorated with cast, applied vignettes of children at play, was made by Gorham and Co., New York, c. 1900. Sadly, the stand has been spoiled by a later inscription dated 1942. £100-£150. The cream jug and sugar basin were made by Tiffany and Co, New York, c. 1880, in the aesthetic style inspired by Japanese art. £400-£500 the pair.

234 Some nineteenth-century christening sets were of great quality, with cast handles decorated with bacchanalian figures. George Adams, London, 1869, £300-£400.

initials of the child to whom they were first given. Plain sets will often sell for approximately fifty percent more than monogrammed specimens.

During the second half of the nineteenth century christening sets became more elaborate. Many included napkin rings and egg cups (see pages 67 and 68) or mugs and bowls (see page 174), and particularly lavish sets might have as many as twelve pieces. These larger sets are more difficult to price, and one would have to add together the values of each component, finally adding on a premium of some thirty percent to allow for the set being complete and in a fitted case.

Miniatures and Toys

Miniature pieces of silver have been manufactured for several centuries throughout Europe. They can be divided into two main groups. First, there are the copies of domestic utensils, their proportions and designs reproduced perfectly to create wonderful scale models. The second type of miniature silver takes the form of groups of human and animal figures. Sometimes decorated with enamelling or studded with precious stones, these pieces were designed for display in the 'cabinets of curiosities' much loved by our ancestors.

For many years it was argued that the first group of miniatures was produced by apprentice silversmiths, the young workmen displaying their talent by the manufacture of fine pieces, often working with metal no thicker than a sheet of paper. A second theory states that miniature items were created for travelling salesmen, enabling them to carry a whole range of samples for prospective clients with less risk of attack

235 Four Queen Anne porringers, each two inches in diameter. These are the most common of early miniatures, turning up for sale quite often. £200-£300 each.

from footpads. Certainly both hypotheses might account for the fact that many British pieces bear only a maker's mark. As they were not intended for sale, there was simply no need to submit them for assay and hallmarking.

While both these theories may contain a grain of truth, today most collectors assume that these delightful specimens were produced primarily as toys for the children of the affluent. Manufactured in two sizes and therefore suitable for both dolls houses and tea parties with larger dolls, they were seen as an ideal way to educate a young girl, instilling lessons in housekeeping while maintaining the child's interest with the sheer delight of handling the delicate copies of her mother's utensils. Curiously, despite their apparent fragility, these tiny pieces have often survived in better condition than their full-size counterparts.

Seventeenth- and eighteenth-century British miniatures are much collected. Often made by specialist silversmiths, many bear one of the two marks registered by David Clayton, a London maker who created many charming pieces including candlesticks, warming pans, and tea and wine services. He entered his marks in 1697 and 1720, and his long career has ensured the survival of a relatively large number of fine toys.

American miniatures of this date are much rarer, and few examples can be seen, even in museums. The earliest piece ever produced in America seems to be a tiny cup measuring just over one inch in height. This was made by John Coney in Boston, probably at the beginning of the eighteenth century. Several other examples of miniature silver made in Boston have been found, but specimens manufactured in other American cities are extremely scarce, standard reference works listing very few examples to tantalize the collector.

236 Selection of George I miniature tea silver c. 1725, the kettle on stand three inches high. Mainly made by David Clayton of London, the two bowls and saucers were produced by John Cann, also a London silversmith. Despite their thin gauge metal, they are sturdy and well-made. £100-£500.

237 Group of dolls' house silver made mainly in Holland, but with British import hallmarks dating the pieces to the turn of the century. Miniature furniture is particularly popular today, and one might well pay £150-£200 for the table and two chairs illustrated.

238 There was a curious fashion in the late nineteenth century for miniature silver shoes, many with pin cushion mounts or forming tiny boxes for trinkets. Once again, most were made in Holland for export to Britain. £50-£500.

Fortunately, numerous charming nineteenth- and twentieth-century miniature pieces still exist, and these are often available for quite small sums of money. Large numbers were produced by both Birmingham and Chester silversmiths, ranging across a wide spectrum of domestic articles. Tiny part-fluted teasets are particularly common, their trays measuring about two and a half inches in length. Many miniatures were not purely decorative, and thousands of animal and bird pin cushions were manufactured at the turn of the century from thin sheet metal. The most common pin cushions found today are those created in the shape of a pig, a baby chicken, or a shoe. These can vary in size, ranging from one to six inches in length. More unusual animal and bird pin cushions are much collected. The choice is wide, and Christies of South Kensington have sold elephants, kangaroos, crocodiles, pug dogs, snails, swans, and owls over the last few years. In March 1987 a rare roller skate pin cushion with revolving wheels was auctioned. Despite considerable bruising and some serious splits this sold for just over £100.

Many silver toys were produced in Holland at the turn of the century, often copying much earlier pieces in style and ornament, and sometimes even reproducing antique hallmarks. They were made primarily for export to Britain, and many bear the initials of Berthold Muller, a German who sponsored their importation, assay, and subsequent distribution to retailers throughout Britain. Pieces of miniature furniture are particularly common, and suites of matching items are much collected. Some of the more elaborate items even have opening doors and sliding drawers, their flat surfaces stamped with simulated wood graining or rococo scrolls and flowers. A pleasure to handle and easy to display in small cabinets or even in tiny room sets, they arouse wonder and delight despite their lack of quality and substance.

239 Turn-of-the-century novelty pin cushions are now in great demand, despite the fact that they are generally badly made, with thin, stamped mounts. Prices would range from £50, for a small chick or pig, up to £250 for a more unusual animal or bird.

240 Edwardian tea and coffee set by C.S.and F.S., Chester, 1904, the tray just under three inches long. Such pieces are still commonly available today. £100-£120.

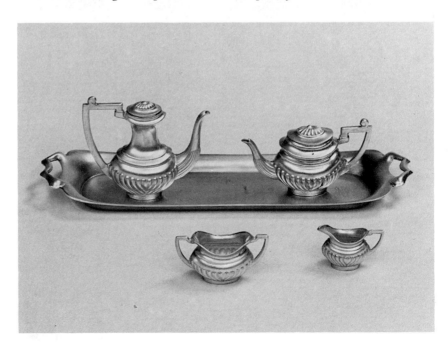

Miscellaneous Pieces for Children

The earliest feeding vessels for children were spout cups. These were lidded baluster-shaped bowls fitted with a slender curved spout, so that a liquid could be poured into the child's mouth with little risk of spillage. Spout cups were made in both Britain and America, but examples are now extremely rare.

Spout cups were replaced by pap boats, small, shallow vessels resembling sauce boats but usually without handles and legs, although some rare American specimens may have these. First made in the early eighteenth century, they were used to give bread soaked in milk or other semi-liquid food to children. By the 1760s most pap boats were made from thinly-rolled silver, and many examples now had applied beaded or gadrooned mounts, serving both to decorate and to strengthen the flimsy edges of the thin metal.

Other curious feeding aids look like curved syphons, with ivory mouth-pieces and applied clips. The clips were designed to hold the device onto the rim of a cup, so that a child could suck up a thin broth or infusion using the curved piece of silver as a straw. Made in pottery as well as in silver, a Wedgwood catalogue circa 1800 describes them as 'sick syphons'. A further variety had a small bowl with hinged cover for ease of cleaning. The bowl was attached to a slender, hollow spout. These small pieces, usually no longer than a large teaspoon, were probably used for dispensing foul-tasting medicines. The narrow spout was inserted through a gap in clenched teeth, and the recalcitrant child could then be dosed with ease. The two types of feeding aid described above are now very expensive.

Although the babies of the wealthy were often breast-fed by 'wet nurses', some women did nurse their own children. Indeed, it was commonly believed that breast-feeding acted as a method of contraception. As a result, some mothers continued to breast-feed for much longer than is usual today. The eighteenth-century silversmiths created some rather curious aids for these women, designing pierced circular discs with

241 Unusual piece made by Rebecca Emes and Edward Barnard, London, 1812. Anachronistic in style, it was presumably commissioned by an old-fashioned client. £600-£800.

242 Rare American spout cup, Edward Winslow, Boston, c. 1720, and an early American mug, John Coney, Boston, c. 1700. Both types of object are much collected, retailing for £8,000-£10,000 and £3,000-£4,000 respectively.

243 *Right:* this rare American baby feeder, made by Edward Lownes, Philadelphia, *c.* 1820, is six and a half inches long. Well-designed and constructed, with nipple, straw, and bottle cap, the latter even has an additional tube to allow air to enter the bottle, as the child sucks out the contents. £1,500-£2,000.

244 *Below:* George III nipple shield by Alexander J.Strahan, London, 1805, just under two and a half inches in diameter. £150-£250.

245 *Far right:* unmarked feeding tube used both for children, and for adult invalids, engraved: 'F.C.Rein and Son, Patentees, inventors and makers, 108 Strand, London'. It dates from the late eighteenth or early nineteenth centuries. £400-£500.

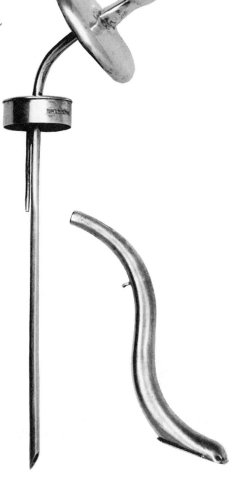

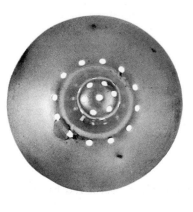

raised centres, closely resembling miniature wine funnel stands (see chapter 4) and measuring one and a half to two inches in diameter. These strange objects are nipple shields, used to protect the sensitive mother from the attentions of an over-zealous toddler. Today, fully-marked Georgian nipple shields sell very well.

The late Victorian era saw the introduction of large numbers of silver and plated money boxes, mainly produced in Birmingham and Chester. Novelty shapes were particularly popular, and one can still find charming, humourous boxes modelled as letter boxes, policemen, or Humpty Dumpty. The more traditional 'piggy bank' always remained in favour and is therefore more readily available. Nevertheless, perfect examples are uncommon.

Finally, small silver brooches designed for children were manufactured in large numbers in the late nineteenth and early twentieth centuries. In America they were usually sold in pairs, and were used to attach the corners of the child's bib to the shoulders of his clothing. Most were simply engraved 'Baby' or 'Darling', although Montgomery Ward and Co. advertised plain gold examples for $1 each in 1895, offering to engrave any name at no extra cost. Their range of silver brooches cost between fifty-seven and seventy cents a pair, although one could also buy gilt brass examples decorated with 'hard blue enamel' for as little as twenty-five cents a pair. Similar brooches were made in large quantities by British silversmiths, the trade based primarily in Birmingham. Several examples are illustrated in an undated late nineteenth century 'Descriptive Wholesale Catalogue with Designs and Prices' produced by J. Langdon Davies and Co. of Bristol Street, Birmingham. These brooches were sensibly provided with a 'protected pin-point'. Marked baby brooches are now comparatively unusual, but one can still find unmarked specimens for very little in many antique fairs and markets.

246 Amusing Edwardian money box, by Henry Wilkinson and Co., Birmingham, 1905, formed as a grotesque figure clutching an umbrella, the base sanctimoniously stamped: 'Always prepared for a rainy day'. £300-£400.

Bibliography

Books of Marks

Belden, Louise Conway, *Marks of American Silversmiths in the Ineson-Bissell Collection*, The University Press of Virginia, 1980

Culme, John, *The Directory of Gold and Silversmiths, Jewellers and Allied Traders, 1838-1914*, Antique Collectors' Club, 1987.

Ensko, Stephen G.C., *American Silversmiths and their Marks*, Dover Publications Inc., published 1948, reprinted 1983

Grimwade, Arthur G., *London Goldsmiths 1697-1837, their Marks and Lives*, Faber and Faber, published 1976, reprinted 1982

Jackson, Sir Charles, *English Goldsmiths and their Marks*, Dover reprint, 1964

Kovel, Ralph M., and Terry H., *A Directory of American Silver, Pewter, and Silver-plate*, Crown Publishers Inc., 1961

Rainwater, Dorothy T., *Encyclopedia of American Silver Manufacture*, third edition revised, Schiffer Publishing Co., 1986

Wyler, Seymour B., *The Book of Old Silver*, Crown Publishers Inc., 1937

General Books

Army and Navy Stores Ltd., *General Price list, 1935-1936*

Bennett, Raymond, *Collecting for Pleasure*, The Bodley Head Ltd., 1969

Birmingham Gold and Silver 1773-1973. Exhibition Catalogue, City Museum and Art Gallery, Birmingham, 1973

Brandon, Sue, *Buttonhooks and Shoehorns*, Shire Publications Ltd., 1984

Brett, Vanessa, *The Sotheby's Directory of Silver 1600-1940*, Sotheby's Publications, 1986

Buhler, Kathryn C., *American Silver 1655-1825 in the Museum of Fine Arts, Boston*, Museum of Fine Arts, Boston, 1972

Butler, Robin and Walkling, Gillian, *The Book of Wine Antiques*, Antique Collectors' Club, 1986

Carpenter, Charles H. Jun., *Gorham Silver, 1831-1981*, Dodd, Mead and Company, 1982

Carpenter, Charles H. Jun., and Carpenter, Mary Grace, *Tiffany Silver*, Dodd, Mead and Company, 1978

de Castres, Elizabeth, *A Collector's Guide to Tea Silver, 1670-1900*, Frederick Muller Ltd, 1977

de Castres, Elizabeth, *A Guide to Collecting Silver*, Bloomsbury Books, 1980

Clayton, Michael, *Christies Pictorial History of English and American Silver,*
    Phaidon·Christies, 1985
Colman Collection of Mustard Pots, Exhibition Catalogue, Victoria and Albert Museum,
    1979
le Corbeiller, Charles, *European and American Snuff Boxes,* Chancellor Press, 1983
Culme, John, *Nineteenth Century Silver,* Country Life Books, 1977
Delieb, Eric, *Investing in Silver,* Corgi, 1970
Delieb, Eric, *Silver Boxes,* Ferndale Editions, 1979
Druitt, Silvia, *Antique Personal Possessions to Collect,* Peerage Books, 1980
Eldred, Edward, *Sampson Mordan and Co.,* Privately-printed monograph, 1986
Fales, Martha Gandy, *Early American Silver,* E.P. Dutton and Co. Inc., 1973
Fennimore, Donald L., *Silver and Pewter,* Alfred A. Knopf, 1984
Harrods, *A selection from Harrods General Catalogue, 1929,* David and Charles, 1985
Henderson, Marjorie, and Wilkinson, Elizabeth, *Cassell's Compendium of Victorian
    Crafts,* Cassell Ltd., 1977
Holland, Margaret, *Silver – An Illustrated Guide to Collecting Silver,* Cathay Books, 1978
Holland, Margaret, *English Provincial Silver,* Arco Publishing Co. Inc., 1971
Hood, Graham, *American Silver,* Praeger Publishers, 1971
Houart, Victor, *Miniature Silver Toys,* Alpine Fine Arts Collection Ltd., 1981
Howe, Bea, *Antiques from the Victorian Home,* B.T. Batsford Ltd., 1973
Johnson, Eleanor, *Thimbles,* Shire Publications Ltd., 1982
Jones, Kenneth Crisp, General Editor, *The Silversmiths of Birmingham and their Marks,
    1750-1980,* NAG Press, 1981
Marshall, John and Willox, Ian, *The Victorian House,* Sidgwick and Jackson, 1986
Matthew Boulton and the Toymakers, Exhibition Catalogue, Goldsmiths Hall, 1982
McClinton, Katharine Morrison, *Collecting American Nineteenth Century Silver,* Charles
    Scribner's Sons, 1968
Meriden Britannia Silver-Plate Treasury, Dover Publications Inc., 1982
Oman, Charles, *English Silversmiths' Work,* HMSO, 1965
Pickford, Ian, *Silver Flatware,* Antique Collectors' Club, 1983
Safford, Frances Gruber, *Colonial Silver in the American Wing,* The Metropolitan
    Museum of Art Bulletin, Summer 1983
Schwartz, Jeri, *Tussie Mussies: Victorian Posey Holders,* Privately-printed catalogue,
    1987
Schwartz, Marvin D., *Collectors' Guide to American Silver,* Bonanza Books, 1975
Stutzenberger, Albert, *American Historical Spoons,* Charles E. Tuttle Company, 1971
Waldron, Peter, *The Price Guide to Antique Silver,* Antique Collectors' Club, 1982
Ward, Barbara McLean, and Ward, Gerald W.R., Editors, *Silver in American Life,* David
    R. Godine, 1979
Watney, Bernard M., and Babbidge, Homer D., *Corkscrews for Collectors,* Sotheby,
    Parke, Bernet. 1981

Glossary

AESTHETIC STYLE: A fashion introduced from Japan in the 1870s, and soon popular both in Britain and America. It was characterized by bright-cut birds, insects, and plants, frosting, and curious fan-shapes

AMORINO: A little cherub, also known as a putto, often used to enliven silver in the rococo period and by the Victorians

ARABESQUES: An intricate woven design of scrolling foliage and flowers

ARMORIAL: A family coat-of-arms, sometimes incorporating a crest

ASSAY: To test a silver alloy, to verify that it comes up to the required standard

BAKELITE: A type of rigid plastic invented in the nineteenth century

BALUSTER: A slender pear-shape, used for such items as finials, candlestick stems, and knife handles

BEADING: An ornamental edging made from tiny half spheres or beads, particularly popular in the late eighteenth century, when it was commonly known as pearling

BRIGHT-CUT: A technique of engraving using a special tool to create polished facets. These catch the light to give an attractive, sparkling effect

BRITANNIA STANDARD: A higher standard of silver with 958 parts of silver alloyed with 42 parts of base metal, mainly copper. This was introduced in 1697, in an attempt to prevent the clipping of coins for the manufacture of silver objects. Britannia Standard silver proved to be too soft, so the practice was discontinued on a large scale in 1720. Numerous pieces in reproduction styles are still made in Britannia Standard

BUFFING: The polishing of silver, usually by machine, to achieve a mirror-like surface. This is harmful to old pieces, as it may remove both hallmarks and patina

CARTOUCHE: A shape left plain to receive an engraving, normally a crest or armorial

CASTING: The creation of an object by pouring molten silver into a mould, often made of sand. Alternatively, the LOST WAX method of casting uses a shape sculpted in wax and then surrounded by a stable material such as plaster. The molten metal is poured into the mould, filling the space left by the wax which melts and runs away. Both methods are used to create solid objects, as well as decorative friezes or components such as feet, spouts, and handles

CELLULOID: An early type of plastic made from camphor and cellulose nitrate

CHASING: Decoration on the surface of an object, using a blunt punch which depresses the background, leaving a raised design. No metal is removed during this process

CUT-CARD: A style of decoration first popular in the late seventeenth century, in which shapes are cut out from thin sheet metal and then soldered onto the body of a piece of silver

DIE-STAMPING: An inexpensive technique, first introduced in the late eighteenth century, used for mass-produced decoration. Hardened steel dies carved with designs were stamped onto sheet silver under great pressure, leaving behind a sharp image which gave the impression of hand-chasing

ELECTRO-PLATE: Base metal, usually a nickel alloy, coated by electrolysis with a thin layer of silver

EMBOSSING: Decoration by raising a design from behind using a blunt punch. No metal is removed during the process. Also called REPOUSSÉ. The end result closely resembles that achieved by chasing

ENAMELLING: Covering the metal with a thin layer of translucent coloured glass

ENGINE-TURNING: Machine-engraving employed to create a regular pattern, often geometrical

ENGRAVING: Decoration by cutting lines in the surface of the silver. Small particles of metal are removed by this technique

ETCHING: Decoration produced using the corrosive effects of acid

FEATHER-EDGE: A style of engraving resembling the barbs of feathers, often applied to the handles of cutlery

FILIGREE: Finely-drawn metal wire formed into elaborate designs

FILLED: Objects made from sheet metal filled with pitch or plaster to add both weight and strength. It is commonly used for knife handles, dressing table pieces, and candlesticks, which may also be described as loaded

FINIAL: A decorative knob on the highest point of an object. This may be baluster or vase-shaped, or formed as a flower

FLATWARE: A general term for cutlery formed from flat sheets of metal

FLUTING: A series of ridges which may extend over part or all of an object. The flutes may be straight or spiralling

FLY-PUNCH: A machine developed in the eighteenth century by the fused plate makers, to ease the task of piercing metal. It soon replaced hand-sawn piercing throughout the industry

FRIEZE: A decorative line or border, often cast separately and then soldered into place

FROSTING: A finely-granulated decorative surface, used to form a contrast with polished silver

FUSED PLATE: A thin sheet of silver fused onto one or both sides of a block of copper. In 1743 Thomas Boulsover of Sheffield discovered that the two metals would react as one, enabling the manufacture of inexpensive pieces which closely resembled solid silver. Although commonly known as old Sheffield plate, the process was also carried out in Birmingham and other cities, both in Britain and on the Continent. It was superseded by the cheaper process of electro-plating in the 1850s

GADROONING: A series of small flutes applied as a border decoration

GILDING: The decoration of silver with a thin coating of gold, hence silver-gilt

GOTHIC: A style of Western architecture prevalent in the twelfth to sixteenth centuries, characterized by pointed arches and simple lines. It was much copied and adapted in later centuries, particularly by the Victorians

GREEK KEY: A regular, geometric design derived from classical architecture, first introduced during the neo-classical period in the eighteenth century and often used for borders or friezes

GUILLOCHE ENAMELLING: The metal is roughened with engine-turning, providing a non-slip surface upon which the enamelling is applied. The engine-turned engraving can often be seen through the translucent glass

HOLLOW WARE: Hollow vessels, such as cups or bowls. The term also describes hollow knife handles

KNOP: See FINIAL

KNOPPED: Decorative swelling, often on a pedestal foot or candlestick

LOADED: See FILLED

MONOGRAM: Two or more initials which overlap, creating a complicated and decorative design

NOZZLE: The part of a candlestick which actually holds the candle. This is usually detachable, for ease of cleaning

PARCEL-GILT: Silver which is partially gilded

PATERA: A circular or oval foliate design introduced in the neo-classical period

PATINA: A surface gloss produced by many years of tarnish, polishing, and use, almost impossible to reproduce

PUTTO: See AMORINO

QUATREFOIL: A four-sided shape similar to a four-leaf clover

RAT-TAIL: A short ridge of silver applied to the back of spoon bowls, mainly to reinforce the join with the handle although some are more elaborate and decorative

REEDING: Strips of narrow grooves, usually used as border decoration

REPOUSSÉ: See EMBOSSING

SATYR: A horned. grotesque figure, used in both rococo and later decoration

SPOT HAMMERING: A decorative technique which leaves behind hammer marks, usually to create a misleading impression of hand workmanship

STERLING STANDARD: An alloy containing 925 parts of silver to 75 parts of base metal, mainly copper. This has long been the most common standard of silver in both Britain and America

STRAPWORK: Applied decoration incorporating scrolling bands of foliage

TREFID-END: A pattern of cutlery, where the end of the handle is shaped into three distinct points

WRIGGLEWORK: Asymmetrical engraving or chasing, creating a texture

Index

Italic figures indicate illustration
numbers

A. B. Ltd (Birmingham) *160*
A. C. (London) *93*
A. H. (London) *170*
Adams, George 35; *20, 21, 32, 40, 234*
Adams, Stephen *44*
Adey Brothers *71*
'aesthetic' style 155; *188, 196, 233*
aide mémoires 154, 155; *197, 212, 214*
Albert pattern *21*
Allan (James) and Co. *45*
'andiron' sugar nips 57; *58*
apostle spoons 23, 31, 49, 51; *13, 18, 23, 53*
apple corers 39; *33*
Art Deco 12, 51, 54, 71, 84, 121, 139, 141, 146, 167; *6, 46, 51, 177*
Art Nouveau 12, 37, 50–51, 54, 93, 99, 120, 162, 164, 171, 174; *15, 36, 55, 111*
ashtray *187*
asparagus tongs 47; *41*
Asprey 84; *135, 158*
auction rooms 17–18; *7*
Avon 153

Bacchanalian pattern 36; *28*
Barker, Susanna *70*
Barnard, Edward *73, 241*
Barnard, Messrs *222*
barometer and clock *151*
basting spoons 43
Bateman, Hester 60; *49*
Bateman, Peter, Ann and William 47, 49, 59, 70, *139*
Bateman, William 20, *204, 222*
beakers
    christening 171–2
    collapsible 172; *224*
bedroom clocks 123; *149*
bells 118–19; *143, 145*
belt buckles 162; *210*
belt clips *212, 214*
belts 162; *212*
'berry' spoons *10*
Bewick, Thomas 166; *208*

bidding 17
Black, Starr and Frost *111*
Black, Starr and Gorham 84
'blind piercing' 65
blotters 122
bonbon dishes 68–71; *2, 12, 74, 75*
Bond Street Silver Galleries 16
'bonnet whisks' 105
bookmarks 126; *137*
bottle collars 90
bottle corks 90
bottle openers 84
bottles
    cologne 97, 99; *109, 110*
    scent 147, 148–53; *189, 190, 191, 192, 194, 195*
    tot 90; *92*
bougie boxes 117; *141*
Boulton, Matthew 85; *131*
bowls, christening 172–4; *225, 226, 227, 231, 233*
boxes
    bougie 117; *141*
    cigar and cigarette 139–41; *175*
    counter 156; *199, 200*
    gaming 156; *199, 200, 202*
    jewellery 100–101; *113*
    match 144
    patch 156–7
    snuff 131–4; *163, 164, 165, 166, 167, 218*
    soap 105; *124, 125*
    spice 79
    stationery 122
    tobacco 130; *161*
    toothpowder 106; *123*
    trinket 100–101; *113, 114, 115*
    watercolour 158; *204*
    writing 107
Bradbury, Thomas and Son *143*
Braham, Joseph *178*
Bramah, Joseph 111, 112
bread fork 46; *39*
bright-cut engraving 79, 82, 133, 138, 147, 156; *203, 222, 232*
'Bristol blue' glass 66, 70, 71, 92
Britannia Standard 23–4
brooches, baby's 183–4

brushes 75, 105
    moustache 135; *170*
    nib 127
    tooth 106; *123*
buckles 161–2, *210, 211*
Buckton, J. *83*
'bun pepperette' 65
Burt, Benjamin 87
'butler's grater *84*
butt selector 156; *202*
butter knives 46; *40*
button-holes 94–5, 96
buttons 166; *208, 209*
buying 14–18

C. and B. (London *180, 188*
C. B. S. (Edinburgh) *169*
C. C. (Birmingham) *118*
C C (Chester) *229*
C. and C. (Chester) *118*
C. C. (London) *143*
C. and Co. (Birmingham) *154*
C. D. (London) *161*
C. E. (London) *222*
C. F. (London) *161*
C. and N. (Birmingham) *196*
C. R. (London) *166*
C. S. and F. S. (Birmingham) *230*
C. S. and F. S. (Chester) *113, 184, 240*
C. and Sons (London) *58*
cabinet 16
caddy shovels 53; *48*
caddy spoons 51–4; *48, 49, 53*
Cafe, John 116; *138*
'cake slices' 75
calendars 125; *152*
candlesticks 119–20; *114*
cane handles *217, 218*
canisters, cigarette 141
Cann, John *236*
capstan inkwells 108, 120; *128, 129*
capstan pepper-mills 66
'car-lamp' inkwells *127*
Carr, Alwyn 141; *175*
carriage clocks 123; *149*
Carrington and Co. *60*
caryatid tapersticks 116

cases
    cheroot 138–9; *173, 174*
    cigarette 139; *171, 172, 176*
    dressing 93–4, 96, 110; *107*
    sovereign 159; *201, 205, 218*
    stamp 159; *205*
    vesta 142–4; *184, 185, 186, 188, 212, 218*
    visiting card 153–5; *196, 197*
Casey, Samuel *225*
Casper, Charles *45*
cast marks 21
casters 62–5; *65*
'castle-top' snuff boxes 134; *164*
'castle-top' visiting card cases *196*
Catchpole and Williams *51*
cauldron salt cellars 61, 62; *68*
Cawdell, William *18*
cayenne pepper spoon 51
Chantier, John *125*
Chapman, John *125*
chased decoration 32, 53, 85; *2*
chatelaines 162–5; *212*
cheese knives 40
cheroot cases 138–9; *173, 174*
chop tongs 47
christening presents 31, 67, 169–74, 177–8; *220–227, 231–4*
churchwarden pipes 129; *159*
cigar boxes 139–41
cigar cutters 141; *178*
cigar stand *183*
cigarette boxes 139–41; *175*
cigarette cases 139; *171, 172, 176*
cigarette holders 141
Clayton, David 179; *236*
cleaning 25–7; *14, 15*
clock and barometer *151*
clocks 123; *149*
coasters 100
coffee spoons 49, 51; *46, 55*
Coles, Albert 155
cologne bottles 97, 99; *109, 110*
Comyns, Wiliam 100, 120, 123; *5, 75, 109, 113, 114, 115, 143, 144, 146, 147, 151, 212*
condiment labels 87; *100*
condiment sets 61–6; *64, 67, 71, 100*

condiment spoons 51; *47*
Coney, John 179; *242*
conversions and alterations 24, 37,
    40, 41, 74, 121; *11*
corks 90
corkscrew and bottle openers 84; *89*
corkscrew and nutmeg grater 81–2;
    90
corkscrews 80–84; *88–93*
cosmetics 97–9
counter boxes 156; *199, 200*
cream jugs *11, 235*
cream pots *121*
Crossley, Richard 20, 47
Crown Perfumery 152, 153; *194*
cruets
    condiment 66; *64, 100*
    egg 68; *73*
crumb scoop 75; *14, 81*
cups
    spout 182; *242*
    tot 91–2
    tumbler 172; *221*
curling tongs 103
cutlery sets 32–5; *23, 26*
    forgeries 23; *13*

D. and F. (Birmingham) *187, 212*
D. and N. (Chester) *230*
Davies, David and Morris 74
De La Rue 112
'de-chasing' 24
Dee, Thomas William *155*
desk equipment 107–27
    bells 118–19; *143, 145*
    blotters 122
    calendars 125; *152*
    candlesticks 119–20; *144*
    clocks 123
    inkstands and inkwells 107–10;
        127–32
    pencils 113–14; *133, 134, 136*
    penknives 110
    pens 110–13, 127; *133, 135*
    seals 117–18, 130; *142*
    sets 123; *129, 148*
    thermometers *150*
    writing box 107
dessert cutlery 36–41; *28–34*
die-stamping 48, 53, 88, 89, 134
dip pens 110–11, 127; *133*
dishes 68–71; *2, 12, 74, 75*
display 28–9; *17*
Dixon, James and Sons *80, 126*
dog-nose spoons 23; *18*
Dominick and Haff *5*
Doulton, Royal 131
dressing-cases 93–4, 96, 110; *107*
dressing-table sets 93–6, 123; *1, 106,
    107, 108*
Drew and Sons *93*
Drinkwater, Sandilands 86
'drum' mustard pots 65
'duck' salt cellars *63*
Dunhills 141, 146; *177*

'Dutch' doll sugar nips 59; *60*
'duty dodgers' 20
'dwarf' candlesticks 120; *144*

E. C. B. (London) *185*
egg cruets 68; *73*
egg scissors *22*
egg servers 75
egg spoons 68
Eley, William 10, 21, 32, 38, 41, 47
Eley, Fearn and Chawner *73*
Elkington and Co, 119, 146; *40, 66,
    143, 162*
Emes, John *39, 141*
Emes, Rebecca *73, 241*
Emes and Barnard *95*
enamelling 139, 142; *171, 172, 175,
    176*
engine-turning 130, 133, 141, 147,
    155
envelopes, stamp 127
étuis 155; *198*

F. D. (Birmingham) *184*
Farley, Charles *221*
'Farrow and Jackson' type corkscrew
    82; *90*
Fearn, William 10, 32, 38, 41, 47, 73
feeding aids 182–3; *241–5*
fiddle pattern 34; *20*
fiddle, thread and shell pattern *21*
fish forks 45; *37, 42*
fish knives and forks 35; *24, 42*
fish servers and slices 44–6; *36, 37,
    38*
flask and cheroot case 90
flasks 90–91; *101, 102*
flatware 32–5, 36, 47–51
    patterns 34; *20, 21, 23, 24*
fly-punch 70
fob seals 117
'folding bow' corkscrew 80–82
folding fork 39
folding fruit knives 37–9; *27*
forgeries 19, 20–25, 41, 55, 56; *11, 12,
    13*
forks 23, 31
    bread 46; *39*
    fish 35, 45; *24, 37, 42*
    folding 39
    pickle *39*
    toasting 46; *39*
    trefid-end *19*
fountain pens 112–13; *135*
Fox, George *104, 226*
Fradley (J. F.) Company 168
fruit knives 37–9; *27, 137*
fruit spoons 37; *10, 23, 55*
fruit strainers 55, 56, 77–9; *87*
funnel stands 86
funnels, wine 85–6; *94, 95*
furniture, miniature 181; *237*
fused plate 69, 133

G. G. (London) *53*

G. R. (London) *52*
G. Y. and Co. (Chester) *145*
gaming boxes 156; *199, 200, 202*
Garden, Philip 83
Gardiner, Baldwin 30
gilding 11, 27
Gillott, Joseph 111
Gladstone bag 94
glove-powderers 95; *104*
glove-stretchers 94, 95, 96
Goldsmiths and Silversmiths
    Company Ltd 55, 78, 82, 132, 226
Goliath pocket watches 123; *149*
'goose egg' ladle 76
Gorham and Co. 174; *116, 223*
Gorham, Webster and Price 165
grape scissors 36
graters
    'butler's' *84*
    nutmeg 79–80, 81–2; *86, 91*
    table *85*

H. and A. (Chester) *184*
H. and H. (Birmingham) *122*
H. M. (Birmingham) *55*
H. S. Ltd (London) *70*
'hair tidies' 99
Hall (Martin) and Co. 21, 37, 73, 227
hallmarks 20–24, 48
Halstead, Benjamin 165
hand-bells 118–19; *143, 145*
hand-mirrors *15, 120*
handbag mounts 167; *214*
handbags 167
Hanoverian pattern 34, 43, 47, 48, 51;
    20, 23
Harding, H and Co. *223*
Harrison, Henry *23, 42*
hat-pin stands 102; *118*
hat-pins 102
Hatden and Gregg *38*
Hawkins, John Isaac 113
Heath, George *173*
Heath and Middleton *66*
Hennell, Robert and David 66, 108; *3*
Herbert (Samuel) and Co. *139*
Higgins, Francis 35; *24, 26, 32, 35*
Hilliard and Thomason *232*
'historicism' 11
horn snuff mulls 135; *169, 170*
Hurt, Jacob *91*
Hutton, Edward *224*
Hutton, William and Sons Ltd 32, 55,
    75, 78, 222

I. H. (London) *41*
I. R. (London) *92*
infusers 56; *53, 54*
initial labels 89; *99*
inscriptions, removal of 19
inkstands 107–8, 116; *130, 131, 132*
inkwells 108–10, 120; *127, 128, 129*
insurance 29

J. D. and W. D. (Chester) *116*

jars
    tobacco 130–1; *162*
    toilet 97–9; *109, 110, 111*
Jenkins, Thomas 97
Jensen, Georg 84
jewellery boxes 100–101; *113*
jockey cap caddy spoon *49*
jug, cream *11, 235*

Kauffmann, Angelica 93
Kempton, Robert *138*
Kidder, James *91*
King, John *18*
Kings pattern 34; *20*
Kirk, Samuel and Son 76
Kirkwood, R. and H. B. *168*
'kitchen pepperette' 65
knife handles 35, 39; *23, 25*
knife rests 74; *23, 80*
knives
    butter 46; *40*
    cheese 40
    fish 35; *24*
    fruit 37–9; *27, 137*
    paper 125–6; *158*
    pistol-handled *23*
    pocket 137
    table *25*

L. and S. (Birmingham) *114*
L. and W. (New York) *223*
La Pierre Manufacturing Co. 76
labels
    condiment 87; *100*
    initial 89; *99*
    wine 86–90; *96–9*
lacquering 27
ladles
    punch 76–7; *83*
    sauce 41, 43
    soup 41, 43, 47
    toddy 77; *83*
Lalique, René 153
Lansing, Jacob 68
letter-openers 125, 126
letters clip *156*
Lias, John and Henry *28, 53*
Liberty and Co. 50, 121; *4*
lighters 144–6; *179, 180, 182*
Linwood, Matthew 88
Lister Brothers *53*
London Silver Vaults 16
Loring, Joseph *220*
lost-wax casting method 21
Lownes, Edward *243*

M. and J. (Birmingham) *129*
Mabie, Todd and Bard 112
Macniven and Cameron 111
magnifying glasses 126; *153, 154, 158*
'maiden-head' spoons *18*
manicure sets 103; *118, 121, 122*
Mappin Brothers *46, 180*
Mappin and Webb *40, 107, 110, 121,
    150, 176*

markets 16
marrow scoops and spoons 40; *29, 30*
martelé silver 174
Mary Cooke Antiques *8*
match boxes 144
Mauser *106, 148*
meerschaum pipes 129, *160*
'melon fluting' 86
menu holders 72-4; *78, 79*
Meriden Britannia Company 67
mesh purses 167; *212*
Meyer, Henry *54*
Mills, Nathaniel 134, 155; *164, 193, 196, 197*
minaudières 139; *177*
miniature pieces 121, 123, 178-81; *120, 235-9*
Minott, Samuel *220, 225*
mirrors *5*
    hand *15, 120*
    miniature *120*
    swivelling *122*
money boxes 183; *246*
Mordan (Sampson) and Co. 113-14, 118, 150, 151, 152, 174; *79, 133, 134, 136, 158, 172, 186, 192, 194*
Mordan and Riddle 113
mote skimmers 54-5, 77; *50*
moustache brushes 135; *170*
moustache spoons 22
mugs 22, 24; *9, 11*
    christening 169-71; *220-3*
    shaving 106
Muller, Berthold 181; *63, 214*
mulls, snuff 135-7; *166, 168, 169, 170*
mustard pots 65-6; *69, 70*
Myers, Myer *211*

nail buffer *121*
napkin rings 67; *72, 227, 231*
naturalism 11
Nelme, Anthony *1*
neo-classical style 11, 69; *2*
Newman, Ebenezer *218*
nib brushes 127
nibs, pen 111, 127
nipple shields 183; *244*
novelty pieces 66, 68, 89, 91, 96, 101, 113-14, 119, 134, 144, 146, 148, 150-1, 168, 172, 176; *127, 134, 136, 140, 145, 156, 166, 185, 186, 188, 191, 230, 239, 246*
nutmeg graters 79-80, 81-2; *86, 90*

O. Ltd (Birmingham) *75*
Old English pattern 34, 44, 47, 48, 49; *20, 49*

P. H. (London) *226*
Palmer, Thomas 110
pap boats 24, 182
paper-knives 125-6; *158*
paperweight and sander *155*
parasols 167-8
patchboxes 156-7

'pebbles', tobacco 130
Pemberton, Samuel 157; *90, 200, 203*
pencil and paper-knife *158*
pencils
    novelty 113-14; *134, 136*
    propelling 113-14; *133, 134, 136*
penknives 110
pens
    'dip' 110-11, 127; *133*
    fountain 112-13; *135*
    quill 110-11
pepper mills 66; *66*
'pepperettes' 65
'perpetual' calendars 125; *152*
Phipps and Robinson 33, 98, 100
photograph frames 74, 120-2; *146, 147*
piano candlesticks 119
pickle forks 39
'picnic' corkscrews 84; *93*
'picture back' spoons 48-9
piercing 54, 62, 65, 69, 77; *87*
pin cushions 181; *239*
pipe case *160*
pipe tampers 130
pipes 129-30; *159, 160*
pistol pencils 113; *114*
pistol-handled knives 23
place card holders 72
Plummer, William 44
Plumpton, Henry *58*
pocket knives *137*
pocket lighters 144-6
pocket vesta cases 144; *184*
pocket watches 123; *149*
Pontifex, Daniel *3*
porringers 172-4; *235*
posy holders 159-61; *206, 207*
pots
    cream *212*
    mustard 65-6; *69, 70*
propelling pencils 113-14; *133, 134, 136*
pudding slice *42*
punch ladles 76-7; *83*
purses 167; *212, 213*

Queens pattern *21, 24*
quill pens 110-11
quizzing-glass *153*

R. C. (Birmingham) *201*
rams' head snuff mulls 137; *168*
Ramsden, Omar 54, 141; *175*
Ramsden and Carr *175*
rattles 174-6; *228, 229, 230*
Rawlins, Charles 89
Rawlins and Sumner 84, *99*
razor strop *126*
regency style 11
Reily and Storer *97*
Rein, F. C. and Son *245*
repairs 19
Revere, Paul 60, 165
ring-trees 101, 102; *117, 118*

rococo style 9, 11, 37, 41, 59; *2, 3, 4*
Rotherham Glass Works 147
S. B. and S. (Birmingham) *79*
S. G. (London) *79*
S. and M. (Birmingham) *108*
S. M. L. Ltd (Birmingham) *144*
S. and S. (Edinburgh) *160*
salt cellars 27, 51, 61-2; *3, 63, 68*
sander and paperweight *155*
sauce ladles 41, 43
savoury cutlery 39-41; *30, 31*
scent bottles 147, 148-53; *189, 190, 191, 192, 194, 195*
scent spray 119
Schaats, Bartholomew *163*
scissors 36; *22, 212*
Scooles, M. *45*
scoops
    crumb 75; *14, 81*
    marrow 40; *29, 30*
    stilton 39-40; *30, 31*
sealing-wax 115-18
    holder 115, 118; *135*
seals 117-18; *142*
selling 18
servers 41-7; *35*
    egg 75
    fish 44-6; *36, 37, 38*
sewing equipment 165-6; *215*
shaving mugs 106
Sheaffer, W. A. 112
shell-fluting 43, 50, 53
shell snuff mulls 135
shoe buckles *211*
shoe-horns 94-5, *96*
shoes, miniature *238*
sifting spoon *28, 53*
Simpkins, William 67
skimmers 54-5; *50*
skirt lifters 166; *216*
slices 44-6, 75; *37, 38, 42*
Smith, Benjamin and James *99*
Smith, Samuel Watton *119, 124*
smoker's companions *181*
snuff boxes 131-4; *163-7, 218*
snuff mulls 135-7; *166, 168, 169, 170*
snuff spoons 137
soap boxes 105; *124, 125*
soup ladles 41, 43, 77
soup spoons 35
souvenir spoons 50; *45*
souvenir thimbles 165
sovereign cases 159; *201, 205, 218*
specimen vases 71; *77*
spice boxes 79
spirit flasks 90-91; *101, 102*
spoons
    apostle 23, 31, 49, 51; *13, 18, 53*
    basting 43
    'berry' *10*
    caddy 51-4; *48, 49, 53*
    christening 177; *227*
    coffee 49, 51; *46, 55*
    condiment 51; *47*
    dog-nose 23; *18*

egg 68
fruit 37; *10, 23, 55*
infusing *53*
'maiden-head' *18*
marrow 40; *29*
mote 54-5, 77; *50*
moustache 22
'picture back' 48-9
sifting *28, 53*
snuff 137
soup 35
souvenir 50; *45*
straining 44
'suckett' *31*
tea 47-51; *4, 43, 44*
spot hammering 141, 174; *231*
spout cups 182; *242*
Stamp, James *221*
stamp boxes 126-7; *157*
stamp cases 159; *205*
stamp envelopes 127
stationery cases 122
steak tongs 47
Stebbings and Co. *223*
Sterling Company *212*
stilton scoops 39-40; *30, 31*
Stockwell, E. H. *64*
storage 27
Storr, Paul 60, 87; *3*
Strahan, Alexander J. *244*
strainers
    fruit 55, 56, 77-9; *87*
    punch 85
    tea 55-6, 85; *51, 52*
straining spoons 44
'suckett spoons' 31
sugar basin *233*
sugar nips 59, 60; *44, 55-60*
sugar tongs 57-60; *57, 59*
swan's head scent bottle *195*

T. D. (London) *120*
T. D. and W. D. (London) *156*
T. R. (London) *221*
T. S. (London) *222*
T. and W. (American) *223*
table grater *85*
table knives 25
table lighters 146; *179, 180, 182*
table mats 75; *82*
table snuff boxes 133; *164*
table snuff mulls 135-7; *168, 170*
tampers, pipe 130
Tanner, John *225*
tapersticks 22, 115-17; *130, 131, 138, 140*
tarnish 26-7
Taylor, Joseph 49, 53, 123, 159, 193, 198
tea and coffee set, miniature *240*
tea infusers 56; *53, 54*
tea services, miniature 181; *236*
tea spoons 47-51; *4, 43, 44*
teething-sticks 175, 176
thermometers, desk *150*

thimbles 165; *215*
tie-pins 102
Tiffany and Co. 37, 84, 168; *76, 79, 101, 116, 233*
toasting fork 46; *39*
tobacco boxes 130; *161*
tobacco jars 130-1; *162*
tobacco 'pebbles' 130
toddy ladles 77; *83*
toilet jars 97-9; *109, 110, 111*
tongs
    asparagus 47; *41*
    curing 103
    sugar 57-60; *57, 59*
tongue scraper 106; *123*
toothbrushes 106; *123*
toothpick boxes 157; *203*
toothpowder box 106; *123*

tot bottles 92; *103*
tot cups 91-2
travelling corkscrews 80-84; *88*
travelling dessert pieces 37-9; *33*
travelling inkwells 110
tray inkstands 107-8; *130, 131*
trefid-end forks *19*
trefoil cruets 66; *64*
trinket boxes 100-101; *113, 114, 115*
trinket trays 100; *116*
trowels 44
tumbler cups 172; *221*

umbrellas 168

vases 71; *77*
Venetian pattern *21*
Vernon, Samuel *225*

vesta cases 142-4; *184, 185, 186, 188, 212, 218*
Vickery, J. C. *127*
vinaigrettes 147-8, 150; *193*
visiting card cases 153-5; *196, 197*

W. A. (Birmingham) *117*
W. C. (London) *70*
Walker and Hall 6, *22*, 40, 79, 80, 150, 180, 196
walking sticks 167-8; *217, 218*
Ward (Montgomery) and Co. 106, 172, 183
Ward, Rowland 146
Warner, Andrew Ellicott *25*
washing 26
watches 123; *149*
watercolour boxes 158; *204*

Waterman, L. E. 112
wax-jacks 115; *139*
whisky tot bottles 92; *103*
whistle rattles 176; *228*
Whiting Manufacturing Co. 35
Wilkes, John 48
Wilkinson, Henry *130, 246*
Willcocks, Richard *18*
Willmore, Joseph 113; *40, 140*
Willmore, Thomas *208*
wine coasters 100
wine funnels 85-6; *94, 95*
wine labels 86-90; *96-9*
writing box 107

Yard-o-Led Pencil Company 114

Zachery, A. and J. *184, 196*